TIMING IS *Almost*

EVERYTHING

12 Steps to Executive Success in Software Management

Roland Racko

Copyright

Contents

Acknowledgment

Special thanks to Ivar Jacobson, the driving force behind SEMAT Essence. The more casual conversations we've had over the last two decades inspired the mindset behind this book. The heated debates we've had have sharpened us both – who could ask for more than that?

Bushels of props to some people who have unwittingly contributed to this book by their sterling examples of what it means to be relentless in the pursuit of software excellence – Ed Yourdon, Tom DeMarco, Meilir Page-Jones, Tom Plum, Steve Weiss, P.J. Plauger. That includes an additional special fist bump to P.J. who counseled, "By the way, try not to write a book that fills a much-needed vacuum."

A very warm and heartfelt gratitude to hundreds and hundreds of public seminar students, magazine column readers, software managers and clients whose frustrations and laments have taught me more about what works and what doesn't than any studying I could have done on my own.

Finally, huge thanks go to Ivy Green whose support made timely publication of this book possible.

Introduction

ATTENTION: CEOs, start-up entrepreneurs, executives.

Is it a burning goal of yours to have a successful, world-class, software project?

Could you also be one of those senior executives who feel that they report to their computers, rather than their computers reporting to them?

Or are you relaxed because information technology projects are running so smoothly that you feel like nobody needs your guidance anymore? If you are in this relaxed group, then this book is likely not for you. You can stop reading, put it down, and gloat about your successes to the person sitting next to you on the airplane.

Since you are still reading, let's speculate that you feel a certain frustration regarding information technology and/or you are curious to know more. And, let us further speculate, that you would like to enhance the influence and control you have over the business value and success of software construction in your company.

GOAL OF THE BOOK

All the equipment you need to enhance that influence and control is in this book. There are 12 precise executive steps. These steps change the timing and influence of your power. This book includes tips, tricks and tools - some old, some new, about the "how" to exert that influence. The book details give you:

- A set of "management-by-query" style of non-geek questions that you can ask yourself and your software team. They are queries that will help guide the team to deliver better business value from your software systems – queries which will engage, inspire and enliven those who report to you

- Critical tactical timing guidance that gives you the best leverage for communicating, adopting and transitioning to the ideas behind each management query

- Jargon-free monitoring tools that deliver precision feedback about your software system's progress that you likely have not yet experienced

- An objective way to diagnose trouble areas in your software development process and ways to improve performance in those areas

- A framework for understanding what has previously prevented your influence from producing the maximum business value from your software systems.

In short, these pages show the non-technical executive (someone having approval control over software development) a new way to corral the software development process in a manner that enhances the business value of the product and the project.

How?

By building on insights you already possess: life experience. The insights used here have always been part of your experience even though that experience has been mostly, if not entirely, non-technical. The book conceptually divides the assertion of executive influence into 12 steps, each of which is strategically-timed. Each step draws on those life insights.

You are not simply reading a handbook on how a largely non-technical executive can successfully manage software teams using strategic timing, but you are also about to learn how to repurpose your best personal insights to achieve maximum business value from your project.

The guiding pages of this book show how to time the following software team actions:

- implementing a "software architecture" as a framework and context to discuss proposed solutions,

- establishing "software floor plans" to describe and critique the software architecture of those proposed solutions,

- creating common terminology between users, stakeholders and developers,

- constructing software components in an ordered way derived from the software floor plans,

- optimizing the context in which to begin the full funding of the project.

These team actions are designed to bridge and reconcile disparate definitions of success that can exist between executive and the team which enhances delivered business value of the project.

AUDIENCE OF THIS BOOK

The principal audience is senior executives, at any level, frustrated by company past experiences with software projects.

Entrepreneurs of start-ups, who suddenly find themselves unexpectedly pummeled by the need for elaborate software systems just to start the business, will also find this book exceptionally valuable. Start-ups often attract passionate, yet unseasoned software talent. The "old-hat" ideas get shortchanged in start-ups because they haven't yet experienced the usefulness of "old-hat" techniques. Reviewing these will avoid some horrendous start-up goofs that would otherwise delay entry into the window of opportunity.

Is there anybody who should put this book down and leave themselves out? Yes.

If you are a theoretician, methodologist, agile fanatic or sensitive to politically incorrect software language, you should run screaming for the exits and remove the battery from your laptop or e-reader before it self-destructs.

INFLUENCE: TIMING AND MAGNITUDE

Influence has two components – timing and magnitude; i.e., *when* the influence is delivered, and the *strength* of that delivery. A major point of this book's ideas is to alter the precise moment in time at which the executive exerts influence.

Typically, an executive expresses influence the first moment that executive presents a software team with a problem to be solved with software. The influence is initiatory in its timing and low key in its magnitude. Presuming the software team is a good one, the team first refines the problem statement and then precisely defines a set of computer system requirements which will act as an effective solution for the opportunity. The executive then exercises a confirmatory influence, saying yes, (or maybe no) to the proposed system.

Influence is generally not exerted with commanding strength by the executive until there is a significant problem to be solved. All too often this takes place after the software team has exerted tremendous effort to accomplish the goals of the executive as the software team understands those goals.

As an example, when the system is finally installed, the executive unleashes great, intense influence to correct an often fabulously disappointing situation as the executive discovers the horrendous gaps that exist between what was desired and what was delivered. Despite the considerable energy made available at this point in time by the executive, the system never quite hits the mark, because making major repairs to a fully constructed system is incredibly expensive and draining. Also, such repair can be politically arduous since the budget is typically exhausted.

In an even more futile waste of energy, the disappointment is typically followed by the executives trying to exhort developers to use the latest tools, techniques, research or methodologies to improve the next software system. Usually, the new exhortations fall largely on deaf ears.

What prevents those exhortations from being successful?

Often developers become numb. They become numb if they experience that the last set of exhortations had insufficient support follow on from the same management team that exhorted them.

Hint: exhortation without thoughtful transition planning and support doesn't work. (We examine ways to correct that failure in step 12.)

This book re-orders the timing point to unleash strong executive influence. Further, it strengthens the confirmatory moment, the early moments of system solution proposal, rather than strengthening the end of the project, when it is nearly always futile and frustrating. The assertion of influence in those initial conversations, using a "management by query" style, triggers a cascade of dynamic positive effects.

The first of these effects aligns the meaning of success for both technical staff and executive. In that initial conversation, both technical staff and executive perceive and define the word "success" differently. They may not always acknowledge that difference. The executive probably thinks of success as meaning the computer system delivers value to the business. The technical team, having more direct experience with the extraordinary complexity inherent in today's systems, thinks differently. They may often only think of success in terms of simply getting the computer system to run at all, by a scheduled delivery date.

To improve the executive's influence over the business value delivered, and to reduce disappointment in the system, what is needed in this conversation is something that will allow *both* definitions of success to operate and flourish concurrently. The resulting operative framework then has a sufficiently common language that is both one of the goals as well as the byproducts of the ideals to which this book is a simple yet useful guide.

As an example of the usefulness of a common language and architecture, consider building a resort home. From the first day of conception through the completion of the home, drawings, floor plans and blueprints are used to guide and coordinate the process. They are a thinking tool, a planning tool, a specification tool, an assembly tool and a communication tool. They are an inseparable part of building a home throughout all phases of construction. In order to function on such a broad scale, they are drawn according to conventions, using common verbal terminologies, which are worldwide construction industry parlance.

Similarly, all manufactured items have drawings for various stages of product development -- the larger Boeing airplanes have more than 100 kinds of floor plan-like drawings. The documents used to describe software have equivalent industry standards. Using the insights of this book, special technical training is not necessary for the executive to evaluate the business value of certain of those software documents and, if necessary, reshape that value.

For some of you, a few of the techniques mentioned in the text may appear to be "old hat" because you have heard about them before. You may be inclined to believe, out of habit, that either they are being used in your company or they were historically used but were experienced as ineffective. You might be tempted to simply dismiss those techniques as "old wine in new bottles." The difference is that this book optimizes the "when" of using those techniques. Additionally, the book shows you how to examine the validity of any historical belief about their effectiveness.

HOW THIS BOOK IS ORGANIZED

Part 1: The Executive Role

Chapter 1 explains what makes software intrinsically difficult. It illustrates that the book's method of questions, used by the executive in a novel way, at the right time, can circumvent those intrinsic difficulties. Additionally, it shows how the tactic of using certain questions can trigger a change in the software team's behavior such that they henceforward successfully master those intrinsic difficulties.

Chapters 2 through 4 detail the "management by query" questions (and appropriate team answers) used in the dialogue between the team and the executive. The questions attack the intrinsic difficulties of software discovered in Chapter 1 and will frequently reset the courses of action the software team will take to deliver improved business value.

To provide the executive and team with a consistent vocabulary during their dialogue, these chapters also introduce the world of the "Essence" software standard from the Object Management Group (see http://www.omg.org). Developed by members from the SEMAT community (see http://www.semat.org), SEMAT developed the proposal for Essence and submitted it to OMG. OMG has adopted it and has declared ownership of it.

Rather than elaborate the full specification of this standard, this book highlights what is useful for the executive. It will strictly avoid many theoretical terms of that standard (undoubtedly evoking howls, boo's and hisses from theoreticians and purists). It also does not "sell" or proselytize Essence nor explain all its historical evolution. The book will, however, show the important way that executives, users, stakeholders and developers reading this book can use and benefit from the utility of the jargon-free aspect of Essence.

Part 2: Making Success Happen

The remainder of the book covers the last of the 12 steps to success in detail: adopting and transitioning to the book ideas. The sum total ideas of this book may be radical for some organizations, or at least different, especially the ideas of Essence or the philosophies behind the "management-by-query" executive style. Without adoption and transition guidance, the value of this book can easily get lost in the chaos that often poses as software project progress.

These final chapters, therefore, provide a plan for adopting and inserting the book ideas into a company and making a smooth transition to them. Some executives, ones who perceive the utility of the executive and team dialogue mentioned earlier, will want to make certain that the dialogue becomes a routine company occurrence. These chapters enable such an objective, even in a worst case scenario – an executive in charge of a medium-sized company which has a software development group described as being in a high state of "anarchy."

According to the Software Engineering Institute, about 75 percent of all companies fit that description. Stated another way, 75 percent of all companies are building software with more effort and frustration than is really required.

Generally, such unfortunate companies have:

- no idea about the precise cost of software bugs or bug repair,

- no continuous monitoring of software quality,

- no one with specific responsibility to look for ways to get extended return on investment from original first-time system building efforts, and

- no one responsible for running an explicit, continuous, formal, scheduled review of the exact manner by which people build the computer systems.

This book shows ways of measuring your company's anarchy (see Chapter 5), so you can compare yourself to that scenario and adjust the transition and insertion process accordingly.

PREREQUISITES FOR THIS BOOK

The book presumes the executive has general management skills. The language of this book is largely non-technical. Every attempt has been made to avoid the use of multi-letter technical acronyms. No particular computer literacy is presumed, although it is helpful if you have enough understanding of your information technology department to be able to write a one-sentence description of each of the major computer systems in your company.

For those technical terms that are used, there is a Glossary for reference whenever we have been constrained to compress a complicated concept into such a one-word technical term. When you finish the book, it is worth studying the Glossary in full, as it will help you get your tongue around a vocabulary that will necessarily become part of your enhanced influence and power.

And now, let us begin to learn the details of management by query and the importance of timing.

PART 1 - THE EXECUTIVE ROLE

1

Does the Past Lie to You

Does this sound familiar? "...and I have this great plan from the software team. It will only cost us 50 million dollars," says your CIO/CTO. What goes through your head? "Damn, another 50 million dollars' worth of grief" or something like that?

Information technology should be invisible. It should be an enabling force that allows you to smoothly service existing business and aggressively absorb new business. You should be able to sit in the boardroom, say to the board of directors that you have just hit the "go" button on the project, and then say to everybody that all of them can sit back and watch the plan successfully unfold.

The plan the CIO proposes is undoubtedly great. Based on past company history however, you might feel that implementation of the plan using computers will likely fall far short. But history is misleading you. You are experiencing a symptom of something else going wrong, not the plan.

What is that something?

In this book you are going to learn the reasons things go wrong. And most importantly, you will learn the 12 steps to set them right. But before we look at all of that, it's useful to understand the crucial, top-level differences between software building and other things about which you are likely very knowledgeable such as sales, marketing, distribution, finance, manufacturing. With that understanding, the logic of the 12 steps will be apparent.

However much like black magic that information technology might seem to you to be, the basic thing going wrong is that information technology is, in fact, currently a very crude technology in most companies. This is true, irrespective of the genius of modern hardware. It is also possible that the behavior of your CIO leads you to believe that software is mysterious rather than crude. Because of that mysteriousness, you pay the CIO good money and then tend to let the CIO alone. But what other part of your business do you let alone? What makes software exempt?

If you can decide to intervene, to raise the level of software construction to somewhere above crude, then software can be changed from an overhead filled with unpleasant surprises to something that is a true enabler of good, profitable business. In the following chapters, you will learn how to raise that level.

LEVERAGE FOR SATISFACTION – THE INCEPTION POWER POINT

Do you have the personal power to raise that level, to stop software from being a torment?

Absolutely yes.

Your point of power is that actual moment when the 50-million-dollar proposal is first being made. Let's call this conversational moment your "inception power point." Do something different in that inception power point and your world will change.

That something different is not about giving new kinds of executive orders, rules or exhortations. Currently, in that moment, you probably ask questions like:

• "What are the features?"

• "When will it be completed?"

- "What is the return on investment?"

- "How long until market availability?"

Those are important questions and you can continue to ask them. However, this book is about getting new results. To get new results, we ask new questions. To that initial conversation, we add some new high-payback questions to that list. The asking of those new questions will send a very loud, unambiguous message to all the people below you.

How will that happen?

In order to answer the new questions, those people will have to think differently and alter their behavior from its prior routine. That behavioral alteration will cause a pervasive, profound change in the way your software supports your business.

What are the questions?

Those questions are part of the 12-step process, and it all begins in Chapter 2. You may be eager to skip ahead to see what they are. If you are eager, go ahead and skip if you like. But come back later when you want to understand just exactly what it is about software that makes it possible for certain questions to cause such profound change. We'll start that understanding by next exploring what makes software so tricky.

THE DISTINCTION THAT MAKES SOFTWARE DIFFERENT

The people in your company are made of atoms. The things they work with day-to-day – smartphones, paper forms, memos, copier machines and so on – are also made of atoms. It's atoms working with atoms. In contrast, information technology is about computer bits, weightless electronic elements living inside wires, working with other computer bits.

People - as atoms - have a property that is extraordinarily different from computer bits. That property is the ability to innovate, to handle exceptions to the rule, to ad-lib, to deal with surprise or emergency, to make up new rules. People do all of this in a matter-of-fact way all day, and generally do so with social grace, intelligence and adaptability. People have the ability to follow business policy and procedure, and yet make extemporaneous judgment calls about an adjustment in the moment if need arises. They have the ability to respond to changes in the weather or marketplace, temporary shortage of resources, and even "bad hair days."

Computer bits have no such innovative abilities.

Computer bits are astonishingly dumb. Bits need direction and counseling. This fundamental difference makes software intrinsically difficult to get right. That difficulty presents an enormous unspoken challenge to a software team; it is a challenge which subverts the team energy in powerful ways and prevents full realization of some other business goals as we'll see in the short discussion below.

Slowly, over time, your information technology team identifies the major replicable and routine portions of the business procedures to be performed. Then they try to predict what adaptive behavior might be needed. The team then expresses all this in terms of bits working with bits. Software developers translate the business policy and exception handling skills of people into fixed rules that bits can do to other bits.

But in a way, it is an oversimplification to call this process a "translation" since fixed rules are not intrinsically innovative. The translation process is more like a simulation -- getting bits to at least partially simulate, at faster speed, what innovative people atoms would do if they had the appropriate resources for whatever was the task at hand.

Getting bits to simulate human ad-libbing is fantastically complicated and difficult. The level of difficulty involved parallels the difficulty of getting a cricket to perform (or simulate) singing "Happy Birthday" instead of chirping and then have the cricket go on to do jazz improvisation on the theme.

Software developers consider themselves wildly successful if they get bits to perform just the more routine, non-innovative aspects of what people atoms do without error. They make guesses about which probable innovative behaviors will occur often enough to warrant trying to codify them and putting them in the system. Those guesses are rarely complete because, by definition, they are about behavior that is intrinsically innovative and spontaneous and occurring within an environment which is itself also changing. In other words, it is often quite enough to just get a computer system to run at all.

Another characteristic of software that makes it inherently difficult is the fact that almost every piece of software is a custom piece of software. The development team is making something that it has never built before. That means the team does not have the conscious competence and experiential nuances that come from having already built the same thing several times. The team, despite elaborate preparations, is essentially exploring new territory to a greater or lesser degree with the inherent inefficiencies of such an exploration.

Given the above points, developers historically tested computer systems to the point of that first success, stopped, cheered wildly and breathed a sigh of relief. Because of the difficulty of getting bits to simulate the business behavior of even a single group of people, programmers rarely looked outside that single group's targeted programmed computer system. Computer System A was developed for Group A without reference to Computer System B being developed later for Group B. It wasn't even thinkable that there could be either routine or adaptive behaviors that were identical across different groups. There rarely was an attempt in the first effort to explore if there was any kind of additional return on the initial translation investment that could be used in the second effort. Systems were developed in isolation from one other, with the above limited definition of success being adequate. This bias is largely still true in contemporary software teams.

LOST - SHARED BUSINESS PRACTICES - IF FOUND, PLEASE RETURN TO OWNER

In simulating the behavior of people atoms into behavior of computer bits, what tended to get lost were behaviors in different company groups of people atoms that were identical across groups. Put another way, because software developers in the past built computer systems one at a time and looked at isolated groups of people in business departments one at a time, there was little attempt to identify business behavior common to the many different departments, procedures or groups of people. There was the unspoken presupposition that every new system was always new territory. The result was that in every new system with its new group of people, there was a certain amount of re-translating of what was, in fact, a similar business behavior. Almost without exception, it was a new translation that occurred for every new system. Thus, we see that not only does constructing software take great effort because it's simulating innovative behavior, but it takes even more effort because teams inadvertently redo a lot of the effort in subsequent projects.

These similar business behaviors, this common life blood, can be an important corporate asset when a company can extract it and save its software expression. It is one of the ways the company can buffer itself from the exuberant creativity and adaptability of humans – define and isolate those activities that are the same. There is tremendous business value there because it represents simulations which do not have to be reinvented. Training those bits once, getting them to simulate the behavior correctly, transmitting that simulation expertise forward to the next team and then exploiting that expertise in every future system makes software take less effort in the long run.

In this book, the forward transmission of expertise from an originating software effort is called "extended return." Extended return is additional payback on the original effort. It shows up as shorter time to market for future systems which utilize that effort. And it imparts greater reliability in every future system. Additionally, organizing all new systems around software containing those shared business practices helps ensure that new systems always deliver at least the minimum value inherent in those practices. When these benefits are realized, software moves closer to the role of a true enabling resource and moves out of the intrusive position it now occupies.

This common blood, which represents shared business practices, was rarely assembled in the past. That failure occurred because it was nobody's explicit job responsibility to collect, archive, catalog, and distribute those computer bits. Additionally, it was nobody's job to explicitly design computer systems so that they had an "architecture," a software floor plan which would support both utilization and preservation of that shared business behavior in software.

ASK NEW QUESTIONS; GET NEW BUSINESS VALUE

To ameliorate the intrinsic difficulties of constructing software we have identified, the questions you, as a high-level executive, need to add at that inception power point, are simply ones that probe discerningly for the existence of an architecture and construction process which:

- supports innovation, adaptability and flexibility in response to user or environmental change both during project construction and after completion,

- preserves and utilizes shared business activities, and

- accounts for the custom nature of software.

You ask questions that demand, as an implicit part of the answer, that the life blood is present in those systems and that it is directed toward the other goals you want. You use questions which probe, in a new way, for high business value, and payback greater than just the routine user functions expected by the stakeholders of the software.

Those questions will be new, and possibly even disarming, to your team the first time they are heard. They are expecting you to ask about features, not value. However, repeated asking of certain kinds of questions about architecture and value, accompanied by an insistence on lucid answers, will forever change your company.

In the next three chapters we will look at 11 steps of this 12-step guide. Each step is a question you ask your team about the software system's value. As well, we will highlight what useful answers sound like.

POINTS TO PONDER

In your company, how much collected shareable software expertise is transmitted forward from one project to the next? How much is lost? If you don't know that, do you know what stops your company from measuring that?

Are your non-software departments like manufacturing or sales better at collecting and sharing common business or technical expertise? If they are, what has stopped the software groups from following that lead? What keeps the software groups exempted from behaving like the other departments?

If there is a forward transmission of shareable expertise in your software teams, in what presentation form is it transmitted? By word of mouth? By standardized documents? By programmers' or developers' code? Do you know if people can easily access and read that presentation? Does anybody pay attention to that which is transmitted forward? What is your measurement for that attention?

Do you expect to get extended return on investment from new business procedures that are created for your current sales or manufacturing or shipping groups? Do you expect to be able to redeploy those procedures if you open up a division in another country? Who is responsible for ensuring that redeployment is possible? What stops your software group from operating in a like manner?

What does your software team do to make software systems adaptable to unexpected user behavior, internal company political change, marketplace change, regulatory change, and hardware change either during project construction or after delivery of the finished project?

2

Exercising Your Power With a Velvet Glove

In this chapter, we cover the first 8 steps of this 12 step guide. Each step is a high payback question about value, which in some way addresses the intrinsic difficulties of building software we highlighted in Chapter 1. You could be wondering if you have to take a degree in Computer Science in order deal with these high payback questions. A college degree is not required. You already ask similar questions in other areas of life or business. Now, you're just going to ask them to your CIO, CTO or other technical staff. They will be a kind of velvet glove covering a dominant hand which coaxes and teases your team into new behavior. First, let's look at an area where you use similar questions routinely to determine value about a prospective purchase. Then we'll demystify software by drawing the parallels to that innate understanding you already have.

SIMPLE QUESTIONS FOR A FAMILIAR SCENE

Suppose you were in the market for a resort cottage in the hills near Tuscany. Nothing elaborate, just a simple place where you can get an occasional but vital recharge. Your resort agent lists off these features: one bedroom, bath, living room, two covered porches, kitchen and special 4 burner stove. Let's say this feature list is acceptable. Then the agent shows you this diagram. See if you think it is a jumble or not.

Figure 2-1: Floor Plan - Resort Cottage

Like it? The diagram instantly portrays a horrible botch-up regarding design of the cottage. The features are all there, just like you wanted, but the value delivered by this cottage is sharply reduced by the way the features were put together. It doesn't matter what the cost of the cottage is, or whether it will be finished on schedule. It doesn't matter how state-of-the-art the 4 burner stove with grill is. Its location in the bedroom might be right for a hyper-chef who wakes up in the middle of the night with ideas, but a bad match for you. It doesn't matter how glowingly the agent portrays your future happiness owning this cottage.

Looking at the diagram you can ask these questions: Does the path between the kitchen work area and stove seem reasonable? Will food items find their way into difficult-to-clean spaces? Can you add another bedroom without compromising privacy issues regarding the bath? Can you add anything without mandating another bath as well?

All of this can be seen and inspected because a readable diagram was available that showed how the features were assembled. And, if every time the agent shows you some new cottage, you make similar questions about the floor plan, it won't take long before the agent learns what you want besides obvious features. The agent gets subtly, almost covertly, trained to understand the kind of value you're after.

At the risk of being obvious, there is an important rule of thumb that can be taken from the resort cottage example before going on. It is this - a superior way to ensure that value gets delivered is to focus on the architecture of a solution, focus on how things work together; focusing exclusively on features of a solution is the least effective way.

Evaluating a resort cottage requires examining both features and value returned. In this same common sense way, examination of features and value drives the kinds of questions you will ask about a software system.

SIMPLE QUESTIONS FOR THE SOFTWARE SCENE

Suppose that Figure 2.2 below is the diagram of the 50-million-dollar system your CIO proposed. It is a Human Resource Policy application designed to allow employees around the world to query a central site for questions about vacations, sick leave, overtime and so on. In this diagram, the bigger square boxes with little square ears are major components of the Human Resource Policy application. The small little boxes attached to the upper left corner of the bigger boxes, the little "ears," are places where something like a part number or other identifying data would be placed if this diagram were produced by your team. (For our discussion purposes in this chapter, the "ears" are left empty.)

Figure 2-2: Software Floor Plan Diagram - Human Resources Query System

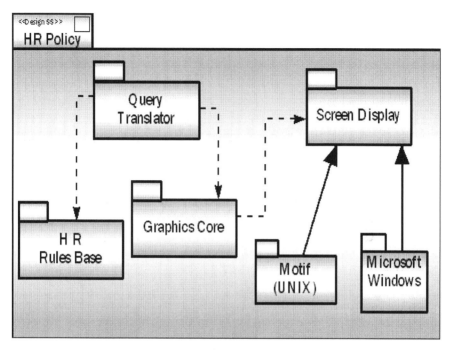

For the purposes of this illustration, the dotted arrows show movement of data or communication between components of the system. For example, the graphics core sends some kind of data to the Screen Display, perhaps special graphic symbols (in the form of bits) that the Human Resources people like. The solid arrows indicate that computing services (bits doing something to bits) are being made available for use by the box that touches the arrowhead. For example, the Screen Display, which constructs the Human Resource screens for query responses, uses the services of Microsoft Windows Operating System to do that construction. The boxes are the core of a component. The arrows are the communication connections or fittings (technicians say "interface") between the components.

That's the basics of navigating this kind of diagram. Your team may use some other diagramming scheme, but it will have similar notions and graphics. They won't call it a "floor plan", since that isn't technical enough for geek-types; they will have another name. Go with it. Summarizing this diagram: there are components and the components provide either services or data to one another. With this insight into the "furniture" of a Software Floor Plan Diagram, we can do the next 8 steps, and that is, form the high payback questions.

QUESTION #1 - What Goes On in Each Box?

The name of each box should give an obvious clue about what the component does in the context of the solution. Fuzzy names, like "network stuff" to use an extreme example, should arouse your suspicion that more homework needs to be done by the team. At a minimum, your team should be able to give you a simple one-sentence description that makes sense to you. Keep asking until you get that sentence. Also, see the glossary definition for "cohesion".

The remainder of the questions in this chapter depends on your having satisfied yourself that you understand the basic function of each component. It is possible that some small number components do not have direct business function but are rather a kind of glue required by the technology at hand to support business functions. That's OK, but you should be clear about which components are of one kind or the other.

Here are some sample answers for question #1:

"The Query Translator converts the user's typed question into a computer form which can be understood by HR Rules Base and Graphics Core."

"The HR Rules Base contains all the human resource policy rules for the company."

"The Graphics Core contains graphs, charts, pictures, company logo, signatures, and so on needed for making the responses visually appealing and presentable."

"The Screen Display makes the pretty pictures on the user's desktop computer or web browser."

"Microsoft Windows is a service provided by Microsoft's software which helps the Screen Display make the pretty pictures on a user's desktop monitor."

"Motif is a service provided by the UNIX software which helps the Screen Display make the pretty pictures for those users connected to UNIX. The system architecture can use either Motif or Microsoft Windows according to the user's input device equipment.

Question #1 is a first probe for good architecture. If simple sentences cannot convey useful meaning about the components, the team doesn't have its arms around this application yet. This question lets the team know that you want to poke around inside this system, see how it is put together and that you will not be satisfied with a simple feature description like "it helps our employees understand our company benefits."

One of our clients was so strongly committed to getting clear responses to this question that he stopped hiring computer science graduates for programmer and developer positions. Instead, he hired English majors and philosophers and then trained them in programming techniques. He did this because that way, he always got systems whose components' descriptions were clear to understand. And more importantly, he got systems that future programmers could understand when they came back later to add modifications to the system.

QUESTION #2 - How much dependency do we have on "X"?

Dependencies on services that are not part of your team's effort can cause havoc if improperly handled. The dishwasher in your resort cottage needs electric services. No electricity, no clean dishes. With this question, you are evaluating the risk the new system will present to your business due to dependencies, whether they are internal or external. "X" in the question above is anything on the diagram that provides services or data to another box. So for this diagram, a question would be "how much dependency do we have on Microsoft's software?" A variation on this question is "what are all the dependencies?"

Every system has dependencies. From your perspective, it is important to evaluate the business risk associated with each of the system dependencies and any limitations it imposes on flexibility and adaptability. If your system is highly dependent on something which is subject to change, frequent upgrade, or is marginally reliable, or composed of new untested technology, then the system presents higher business risk. So this question is an explicit probe about business risk.

Good answers are something like "we have isolated our strongest dependency to 3 Microsoft connecting points which are among the most stable ones in Microsoft's marketing history." The answer shows that the team has been giving thought to minimizing dependency as opposed to wantonly using every possible connection, bell and whistle that might be alluring or glitzy. A primary art of system architecture design is minimizing dependencies.

Dependencies aren't just about services or data provided by components. Quality of service, often called the "service level agreement", is also a kind of dependency. For example, many systems that include a network will have a concern about "bandwidth," the number of bits that can be carried on the wires or fiber optics of the networks. Your questions about dependencies should probe for quality of service levels and fallback plans when service levels are thrown awry because of a wobbling satellite or severed fiber optic cable. In the Human Resources example, any arrow might potentially be implemented as part of a network. There are no universal answers here, except the one that, historically, it seems a company can never have too much bandwidth or too much network fallback.

QUESTION #3 - Which dependencies have we chosen to insulate the system from, what factors led to those choices instead of others and how have we done that?

In the resort cottage, an architect can choose to build the cottage for summer use only or for both winter and summer use. One of the obvious ways to build for both seasons is to make the outside walls thick enough, so that a barrier material can be placed inside the wall to protect against winter cold. The architect could also protect against loss of electric power by including a portable power generator in the cottage appliance wiring circuit, especially if the architect has trumpeted that this cottage is an "all-electric" design. Each choice has an additional cost, but reduces certain kinds of risk or dependency.

Designers of computer systems have the option to insulate the system components shown in the Software Floor Plan Diagram in similar ways. If you don't ask them about such insulation, their habitual choice will probably be to provide minimal insulation in order to keep overall operating and system construction costs down. The company culture may also subtly encourage developers to never try to insulate, since it takes extra development time to evaluate the trade-offs. They will be most tempted to follow the "never-try" habit if the perceived unspoken management priorities have historically seemed to favor meeting the delivery schedule above all goals. So this question gives your team permission to undertake a thoughtful evaluation of ways to minimize the impact of change that could occur in critical dependencies. We will discuss a formal document, the VoxDoc, which your team can build to capture change impact for one and all to see in Chapter 8.

A sample thoughtful answer to this question is something like "we know that the HR Rules Base is in great flux. Policy is revised sometimes as much as twice a year to keep up with competitive employment offerings and our own desire to offer maximum value to our employees. So we have built a little stabilizing filter that sits between the query translator and the rules base. It presents an unchanging face to the query translator and messages rules so that they always look the same to the translator even if the rules are changing underfoot. We chose to insulate only the dependency with the greatest amount of historical change history and are crossing our fingers that the rate of change of everything else stays as small as it has been historically. The stabilizing filter should handle even changes to federally mandated medical policy."

QUESTION #4 - What is the performance cost of the insulation?

Insulation in computer systems has at least two kinds of cost. There is a design and build cost that is a one-time affair which occurs during system construction. The second kind of cost is the effect on system performance (usually speed) that the insulation exacts as the system runs in operation. The insulation will require some computer resources to do its insulating, thus degrading to some degree, overall system responsiveness. This question probes that impact.

Here is the structure of a satisfactory answer for the earlier stabilizing filter: "There is about a 2 percent performance penalty for that stabilizing filter for query loads as high as 1000 queries per minute. It translates into an additional .5 second delay in web browser response." There are no magic numbers for performance degradation values here, but it should be rationally related to the underlying main business requirements and user experience expectations. Often, that means a smallish performance penalty is tolerable. If it is not relatively small compared to resources needed by other components, then there is risk that the system will collapse under unexpected heavy loads. A special performance engineering group may be required, if you do not already have one, to optimally balance insulation resources requirements against other business requirements.

QUESTION #5 - Where do we insulate against changes in government regulations, competitive trends, marketplace trends, etc.?

The architect who designed your resort cottage took into account local, regional, and possibly national building regulations and codes. If he was any good at all, the architect figured into his thinking, trends that he saw happening in those regulations or zoning practice trends which might affect the future serviceability of the cottage.

In a similar way, this question probes for dependencies or assumptions which could be conceivably permeating all components, dependencies which are not related to the arrows in the Software Floor Plan Diagram. To prepare for this question, you, the non-technical executive, should speculate on all the things in the business context you are aware of that might give your business a rough ride over the next several years. It is generally not cost effective to design computer systems which are insulated against every conceivable business contingency that could happen. But the team will take their design priorities from those areas which you scrutinize.

Satisfactory answers would point to specific components on the Software Floor Plan Diagram that performed the insulation against the external business risk trends that are important to you. There may be system speed degradation for that insulation as was mentioned in question #4. Such degradation potential is also worth examining and is another thing called out in the VoxDoc alluded to earlier.

QUESTION #6 - What happens if we change hardware or network components?

Systems can be built in one of two ways: either critically dependent on one-of-a-kind hardware features or, alternatively, built with standardized fittings into which arbitrary hardware can be plugged. "Fitting" here, means the mechanical plugs and electrical signal specifications which need to be common between two components in order for them to work well together. Although there is a spectrum of choices between these two poles, the speed of technological development and the voraciousness of computer user appetites argue heavily towards emphasizing standardized fittings for hardware.

Left to their own priorities, teams frequently choose making systems tightly dependent on proprietary hardware features, using unique fittings rather than standardized ones, in order to wring out maximum performance from the hardware. That behavior is an easy first choice if the special hardware appears to have lower capital costs.

This first easy choice is a kind of specialization of the system which adapts it to the specific hardware in ways that are typically difficult to reverse. When new demands require a later version or faster hardware, that reversal has to be done after all. The undoing of the specialization is costly and time-consuming above the cost of the later version hardware. To outside stakeholders, this effort is frustrating because it apparently adds no new functional value. A key shorthand word which technicians have when discussing this issue is "portability" - high portability means easy adaptability to new hardware, operating systems, browsers, smart phone devices, and so on. So another way to ask the question is something like "how portable is the system software?"

Your team should be able to point to those components, if any, which have been specialized or adapted to particular hardware, devices, network electronics and so on. They should have a well-developed rationale for making those choices rather than more portable choices. And they should also have developed costs associated with being more independent of those specializations so a rational discussion of the near-term versus long-term risks can be evaluated.

A thoughtful answer to question #6 is - "the components feeding the Screen Display, Motif and Microsoft Windows, are the only hardware dependent components. Because we have already organized the Screen Display to accept either of those two, we are, in fact, ready for even a third or any possibility. Geez, Boss, we could connect to a pop-up toaster if we had to."

QUESTION #7 - What happens if we add a new line of business such as Y?

Your team should be able to point to components on the diagram which might be affected by adding a new business line. In all fairness, if the new line of business, "Y", is not something of which the team might have been previously aware, they may need some time to answer this question. In any event, beware of system architectures where the majority of components are affected by such a change. The likelihood is high that such architecture has not yet been refined to the point where the real core of your company's life blood has been found. For the HR Policy System, a good answer would be - "we only need to add some new rules to the H R Rules Base component."

All the previous questions probed to determine if the features of the system would continue to deliver value in spite of perturbations in the environment. They probed how the system was put together in an effort to see if rework of the system, for whatever reason during development or after, was as easy as possible.

QUESTION #8 - What happens if we want to share this system with another division (or company)?

This question probes for extended return on investment. It asks the team to identify components that can be shared by non-local systems. This question probes for company life blood, the bits that have utility across company boundaries, bits representing accumulated expertise transmissible to the next generation of system developers.

If you feel in a particularly puckish and provocative mood, point to the Software Floor Plan Diagram and phrase the question this way, "which of those components can we put in software inventory?" No CEO, no high-level executive has ever put this question this way before. Your team will look at you dazed, perhaps as if you had spoken Sanskrit or twelfth century Gaelic. Just continue, "after all, John Deere Tractor Company has tractor seats in inventory, what stops us from having software components in inventory?"

Here is an exemplary answer to the question - "We've identified that there are patterns in the way different company divisions use graphic symbols. There are four different patterns. By plugging the appropriate pattern into the Graphics Core component, we can get extended return from at least five future systems that are planned in the other divisions. That makes the Graphics Core component an inventory item."

Of course, it is possible that the answer you get is a response to the "what stops us" part of your question. In other words, your people actually delineate the present roadblocks to getting extended return on software. We will talk more about getting extended return in later parts of this book.

The questions of this chapter can provoke answers like "we can't do that" or "it can't be done." While that may be true sometimes in the course of a company's software process, it rarely is as definitive a statement as the strength of the voice tone of the answerer might imply. Architects and team leaders generally are very high integrity people and take great pride in their art, but can be conservative because of past projects that went bad. So they are reluctant to go out on a limb and support an idea which they feel will have chancy success. Often, an architect will say it can't be done when what he really means is that he personally has not done it himself three times before. Or he may say that it's impossible because he feels the cost will be alarming.

Don't stop probing when you hear the phrase "it can't be done." But never ask "why" it can't be done. Using that word "why" will typically get you rationalization, feelings, opinions or justification which then leads to debate rather than progress. Instead, like the software inventory question above, your most useful response is "well, what stops us from doing it?" or "what stops it from being possible?" or even "when did you know it can't be done?" These alternatives to "why" will often open the way to a more objective discussion which will enable the impossibility to be resolved in a surprisingly delightful manner. (We rarely use "why" in that way in this book.)

In the next chapter we will look at guidance steps 9 and 10. They will tell you the way in which the activities of building the system are adding to or reducing the risk of increased software development costs and effort. In particular, we will look at whether it is useful for your team to think heroically.

POINTS TO PONDER

Has your team ever produced a drawing that was supposed to depict architecture? What purpose did they intend the drawing to be used for? Did its purpose include evaluating dependencies? If so, were the dependencies obvious in the diagram, or were only the features obvious?

How much of the computer system development cost has to be expended now before you know what the dependencies are? (Chapter 4 will discuss this question.) As a percentage of total development cost, does that cost parallel the percentage that needs to be spent in other company divisions to identify critical dependencies, divisions such as manufacturing, sales, engineering, or finance?

Do you have in place an inventory system for developer software components that is as sophisticated, clean and as well-financed as the inventory control procedures in other parts of your company? If not, what would stop you from appointing someone with sufficient authority and budget to make that happen?

3

More Glove Work

T he previous chapter showed you the 8 steps to use with an architectural software floor plan representation to put yourself back in control of the business value of your systems before a project gets seriously started. With those questions you begin to change how everyone perceives your interests. Your questions exert appropriate new force to align your inner business vision with your staff's vision in detailed ways not done before. Steps 9 and 10 of this chapter probe the actual software construction process. They coax your team into assembling the pieces and parts of the human behavioral simulation they are building in a manner that accounts for the custom nature of software we identified in Chapter 1.

After a project starts, there is a subtle enemy that works against that business value during the software construction process. That force conspires to prevent or delay the literal construction of the system, thereby diminishing the value you worked so hard to win with the earlier questions. Ordinarily, you shouldn't have to concern yourself about the details of the system's software construction process. However, you are in a unique position to use your power to conquer this enemy with a few simple questions.

The enemy is the human tendency to "bite off more than you can chew" when software teams estimate the time required to build custom systems that simulate or respond to human adaptability and innovation. Enthusiastic software teams can easily get infected by this devil. There are certain moments, though, where you can exert your leverage and ask the probing questions which will still this devil. We'll first take a bird's eye view of how this can happen.

INCREMENTAL DELIVERY OF SOFTWARE

In the pre-Civil War days of programming, when men were men, and women were, well, not much seen out in the programming hinterlands, cowboy coders ruled the range. Cowboy coders started a project by writing the first line of code and kept on going until they came to the end of the trail. They needed only to know code syntax and the business problem. Experts decried such cowboys of course, and talked about the need for software discipline, but on the whole, people considered the notion of software discipline to be an oxymoron. Instead, they opted for long hours and splashy heroism, keyboards strapped to their sides, ready for a quick draw at the whisper of a CPU fan.

The cowboy coder approach was tolerable for the first small custom software projects. But the business world's complexity dashed this originally simplistic approach. And we can't ignore the "exuberant creativity" of Goliath vendors of programmer development tools seemingly bent on maintaining market share by short-term product manipulation—usually bolstered by overwrought advertising hype. So what's a cowboy—or cowgirl—to do? For steps 9 and 10 the answer is "incremental delivery."

Incremental delivery, as used here, means software being constructed in small pieces at a time in a formally decided order. Well, of course, everything is built up from small pieces. In the case of software, the order in which the pieces are assembled can have many options. It turns out that these ordering choices have different consequences. Sounds like a small point. It isn't.

In the resort cottage of the prior chapter, the building contractor conceivably could have started construction with the northeast corner of the building, gradually adding timbers, wall board, plaster and plumbing as he worked his way diagonally to the southwest corner of the cottage. Such a method is ludicrous, would be laughed at by everybody and perhaps the French would have used the word "dérisoire." Historically, many companies still tend to build software in the cowboy fashion mentioned above. In this sort of "high-anarchy" environment, the team starts where it seems possible to start and just keeps adding pieces until everything is completely in place or the budget is hugely overrun, whichever happens first.

Imagine that you were concerned about the water supply of your cottage, the cistern which was to hold winter rains and the plumbing. Further, because of some spur-of-the-moment travel plans, you knew that you would be in the vicinity of your cottage earlier than the scheduled cottage completion date. In that circumstance, you might instruct the contractor to give emphasis to finishing early, these plumbing aspects that you wanted to verify. Effectively you asked the contractor to finish an increment of construction in a special order because of risk associated with a feature. This is a request that was not otherwise relevant to general cottage construction issues. Depending on circumstances, there could be many such reasons to alter the order in which the various pieces of the cottage were to be assembled.

In any new computer system, there will be some areas of innovation, areas where new things are being tried. These new things will present risk. It could be risk from new hardware, new software procedures, or even the political risk inherent in the attempt to please a new group of customers or stakeholders.

Your team's software building process should be organized to identify, in the early stages of system development, all the significant increments. Your team may have already identified increments and tell you that is because they are "using Agile methodology" or whatever is the latest software development process "brand." However, this book is about timing. So let's look at sizing as well as prioritizing the timing of those increments for optimum priority according to perceived business, technical or political risk.

The drawing below is a simple depiction of software team work activities for system building with "time" in months proceeding from left to right. They do not begin all at once as shown by their leftmost endpoint. They do not have all the same amount of hours as shown by their respective heights. Each activity is quite distinct in the types of skills needed and the outputs produced.

Figure 3-1: Allocation of Effort Over Time

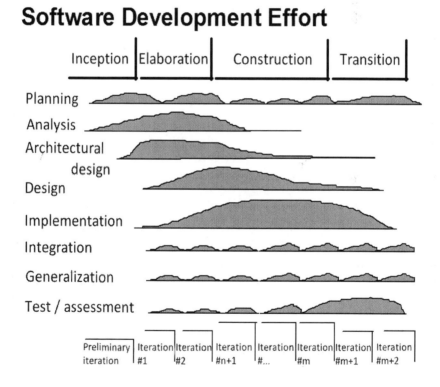

"Planning" is a largely administrative activity concerned with scheduling resources.

"Analysis" is fundamentally investigative. Analysis is the discovery of significant system increments, features, interactions with existing systems, customer or user preferences, etc. that are necessary to define the meaning of success for the system.

"Architecture design" takes the work product of analysis and divides it up into the major system components of the computer solution. It illuminates the way in which major components of the finished system will be assembled together and creates the architectural floor plan which expresses those choices.

"Design" elaborates the internal details of the major components.

"Implementation" is the activity that programmers do, namely writing software code in some language like JAVA or C++ or C# or HTML or whatever combination is appropriate.

"Integration" is the gluing together of the programmer products, an activity which is similar to that of a building contractor attaching a door frame to a wall.

"Generalization" is the activity of examining the components for extended return potential or reworking code to get it.

"Test / Assessment" is the activity where assembled programmer products are tested for correct functioning together. More often, this activity also includes evaluation by the ultimate user of the system.

These work activity labels are probably similar to names your team already uses. Each of these work activities has a bumpy shape in the figure; the height of each bump is an approximation of the relative amount of each kind of activity occurring at any particular point in time.

_*

Across the top of the figure are four major work stages of building software systems. Each of these stages may require some or all of the skills and activities described above.

"Inception" is the feasibility study stage.

"Elaboration" takes the work product of the inception stage and turns it into an architecture. The architecture is shaped according the larger goals of the company, including the goal of extended return and adaptability.

"Construction" is the stage where the bulk of the architecture is translated into bits (often bits which simulate human behavior).

"Transition" is all the various activities associated with giving a completed working system to the ultimate user.

Again, the names of these stages probably have quite similar labels for your team. (We will look at these work stages from another perspective in Chapter 4 when we discuss the question of "where are we?")

Along the bottom of the figure there is written "preliminary iteration," "iteration # 1," "iteration # 2," etc. These are the time intervals during which a system increment is built, with the first increment, "preliminary iteration" being built, including such things as coding and testing, towards the end of the major stage named "inception." The use of the word "iteration" implies that there are mini-stages of elaboration, construction and possibly transition are being done during the increment period.

Ideally, each relatively small piece of the entire system is being designed and translated into something that runs and can be demonstrated to the ultimate user. Each increment is designed so that it piggy-backs on the success of the prior increment in such a way that the composite can be operated as a demonstration of (partial) completion. Each new demonstration shows an ever increasing richness of running system features. This occurs because each increment is accompanied by an appropriate amount of "integration" and "test / assessment." With this initial understanding of the incremental nature of the software building process, we can look at the next of the steps in their question.

QUESTION #9 - What are the system increments, in what order are we going to assemble them and what is the benefit of that particular order?

There are at least four kinds of business risk in computer systems:

- market place risk - how soon can the software / hardware be marketed or deployed,

- political risk - will the ultimate user be pleased (typically for in-house software projects),

- hardware risk - risk associated with immature hardware or technology that is otherwise new to the development team, and

- software risk - risk associated with the fittings between components or the algorithmic procedures within components.

There could, of course, be risks you would like to add to this list. For example, there may be over-budget funding risks. Feel free to add risks appropriate to your project.

Acceptable answers to this question involve trade-offs among all these risks. However, in keeping our focus on timing, structure increments so the highest risks are taken earliest in the project.

What is the advantage of that?

When the highest risks are timed to be tested and assessed in the earliest increments, you get a twofold advantage:

- there is the longest time to recover from a problem found in the high risk area as there is still the bulk of the project calendar which is as yet unused, and

- the riskiest aspects of the system get the largest amount of overall testing, since they are continually retested during subsequent increment tests.

Here is an iteration choices answer regarding the Human Resources application of the previous chapter. A thoughtful answer is followed by the risk being managed enclosed in parentheses:

"We've decided that the preliminary iteration should contain enough of the Screen Display and Graphics Core and Motif such that we can show some sample screens to the user to verify some of our beliefs about the way the user interacts with the system (political risk). That way we can gain some early user rapport, as well, since our past history with the user has been problematic (political risk). Iteration #1 will build on that by adding enough of the Query Translator to test out that insulation we called the stabilizing filter (software risk). We want to get the stabilizing filter up early so that it is tested in every successive iteration because we are strongly counting on it to insulate against changes to the HR Rules Base (market forces risk). According to our environment volatility research (see Chapter 8, the VoxDoc), we expect at least two real unexpected alterations from the human resources department to the Rules Base while we are developing the system. So we'll get a real time challenge to our insulation ideas (software risk). Iteration #2 will add the Rules Base to the network to see if we can handle a large number of queries (hardware risk). In iteration #3 we will..."

If software were always built entirely from standard parts with known interactions, the value of incremental delivery would be minimal. But because software is essentially custom-built, the size of an increment can almost never be too small. In general, each increment should encompass only one item of risk. Increments that test more than one item of risk are too large. In the next section, we examine what makes this so.

THE END OF HEROICS

What happens in your company when people see the lights burning in the software development department after hours? Does anybody notice? Or has everyone become numb to this experience?

If the lights were burning late in any other department and this phenomenon occurred frequently, there would be investigations, inquiries, and reassignment of resources until the problem went away. Somehow this examination doesn't seem to happen in the world of software systems.

How does the software industry somehow give itself permission to exempt itself from this scrutiny?

We call this kind of late night activity "heroic programming." The word "heroic" is used sardonically here -- a jab at the frantic, pizza and caffeine-sustained efforts by which programming teams tend to deliver software systems.

We do not consider any heroic programming ideal. In any other discipline, routine overtime would be viewed as a sign of bad management or ill-appropriated resources. Heroic programming is a sign of something amiss, but what? The kindest thing we could say about this type of programming is that historically, it has given programmers an opportunity to feel special, to feel alive in an unmistakable, adrenaline-buttressed way.

The incremental approach to software construction we have been talking about is anti-adrenaline. The incremental approach works to eliminate the need for heroics. We believe that a major cause of heroics is the difficulty of doing "system integration" using incremental construction sequences which have a high level of anarchy (we speak more about anarchy in Chapter 5). An example of such high-anarchy tactics is to assemble and test together a multiplicity of apparently individually correct components all at one time. When teams operate that way and an error is found, the error of necessity could be in a multiplicity of places. If there were five components being put together at once, the error could be in the fittings between all five, just four, just three or just two. But the team does not know which combination without further forensic work: which five, which four, which three, which two and so on.

With this kind of uncertainty, there will be an inherently unpredictable amount of detective work to locate the error(s), the place(s) where the fitting was inexact or just plain wrong. This detective work must be done before any actual repair can be made and must be done in addition to that repair. Its unpredictable duration means that nobody could have accurately estimated the total detective work effort, i.e. the calendar time and costs, required for all the system integration activities.

Of course people know that project estimates are inexact, so they often build in slop factors. But somehow, these slop factors are always insufficient in accounting for this detective time. That insufficiency is the precursor to heroics.

When only one component, at a time, is connected to the current assembled working pieces, detective work is drastically reduced. What makes this true? When a team assembles a system one component at a time, an error, should one be exhibited, is most likely located in either the fitting itself, what we call the "interface", or located inside the piece being newly fitted (the component). Minimal or no forensic detective work is needed to find the location of the error, no slop factor is needed, and no heroics are needed to make up for the lack of a proper slop factor. By reducing detective time to zero, we have eliminated one of the things that historically have made software intrinsically difficult. All of this brings us to the question of the next step.

QUESTION #10 - Is there anything stopping us from doing the integration and test/assessment on small (or smaller) increments rather than large?

The answer should, of course, be "nothing is stopping us." However, if there is something that is an impediment, question #10 will have brought a seemingly incidental detail to the level where it can be addressed early in the project and where effective resources can be applied. Applying the needed resources to make small increments also leaves your team in the very desirable position of always being able to deliver something that at least partially works should some political or marketplace emergency require an early delivery of the system. Naturally, all of the features might not be in place in that partial system. However, when building a system with small increments in this way, your team will never be in the embarrassing situation of saying "it's 95% done, boss" but having nothing at all that actually runs.

If you don't perform steps #9 and #10, teams in high-anarchy companies will habitually build large increments. They will tend to bite off more than they can chew. They will tend to build those increments in order of technically easiest increments first, or the increments which "get something breathing" however trivial. They will tend to put off all integration till last. In other words, they will take the most risk towards the end of the project when there is the least time and user/stakeholder patience available for recovery. A prominent software company, a former client, poured 200 million dollars down the drain with the same ease as one would empty a bottle of Pepsi. This occurred because they failed to ask question #10 early on in the project. As a result, they had to abandon 4 of 5 major subsystems because the late integration revealed insurmountable problems coordinating aspects of those 4 that had gotten out of synchronization with each of the other subsystems. Having none or few small working increments of the 4 subsystems additionally left them without any user enthusiasm for supplemental funding.

One last point. A side effect of the elimination of heroics is that certain people, addicted to late night pizza, cola, or adrenaline, may feel that the lack of anarchy makes your company boring -- so they quit. Perhaps it tames their inner cowboy too much. We trust that this will be taken as a delightful event.

In performing these 10 steps we have used a Software Floor Plan Diagram. Your team may have a special name for an equivalent representation. You do not have to learn to personally draw any of these (your staff makes the drawings) and you only really need to be able to read the local company equivalent. After all, as a purchaser of a vacation resort you would not be expected to draw the architectural blueprints to scale for that resort.

If you are not getting the kinds of answers you can understand or are nervous that your questions are coming across as repetitive and parrot like or stilted, then go to TimingIsAlmostEverything.com/hpquestions to download a PDF of alternate ways and suggested improvisations on the 10 high-payback questions of these first 10 steps – shorter variations, longer, less formal and so on. Also see Appendix 1.

There is one more step to take before fully funding a project. While the project might pass all the tests you posed about the features, design and construction, you need to ask the question "are we actually ready to start?" The answer is as important as getting the proper start foundation in building the resort or proper start position running a foot race. The next chapter will explore the step you take to tell if the timing is right for your team to begin the project.

POINTS TO PONDER

How does your team traditionally choose the order in which it builds system components? Does the team have a specific risk minimizing agenda and priority? How does that priority mesh with yours?

What formal development process or "methodology" does your company use today? To what degree do developers follow it? How do you know? Why do they think it provides value? Can you/they measure that value? Is there more than one "methodology" in use by different teams? Does that confuse you or otherwise make executive decisions more problematic? Does anyone review the effectiveness of each of the methodologies?

Is there a formal way to improve the software construction process based on learned experience? What process is used by your competitors to improve their software construction process?

4

Where Are We Now?

The previous 10 steps showed you how to use your power, timing it carefully at the beginning of a project. You used questions, diagrams or other architectural representations, to shape the system value as well as shape the most effective way to order the construction of system components. You put yourself back in control of the business value of your systems by timing those right questions.

There is one more step, also at the beginning of a project, which you can use to exert high-leverage influence.

This step 11 is also a question, but one that is asked seven different ways. It is a question asked about the core elements of the system development process your team will use, rather than questions about the finished piece of software. It is asked about the things software teams always do, the things that come together to produce a finished piece of software. The contents of this chapter that elaborate this special question are detailed – and that level of detail might initially seem a trifle overwhelming. Take your time. Read through the material a couple times and let it marinate. Then use the next chapter to make some timing decisions about how you are going to employ what you learned from the first 11 steps.

Recall that we have been focusing on the importance of timing when exercising your power. With this chapter's special question, we are inquiring: "Is this the right time to fund this project?" We are asking "Are all things so well enough along that now is the optimal time to settle the money issues?"

You can make this inquiry in the right way when you understand exactly what those core elements of a software development process are. From the helicopter view, in every software project, there are seven core elements:

- the opportunity -- the rationale or reason the company wants to develop or change a software system,

- the stakeholders -- the people who affect or will be affected by the system,

- the requirements -- what must the system do to exploit or develop the opportunity and satisfy the stakeholders,

- the system -- a collection of software, hardware and data that provides the value that somebody is paying for (either the stakeholder or possibly the marketplace),

- the team -- all the people actively engaged in the construction and work to build the system,

- the work itself -- the mental and physical activity expended in order to achieve the system, and

- a way of working -- a set of rules, tools and procedures that the team uses to guide the work and its progress.

The development process for all software systems, anywhere and for all time, will have at least these core elements. Certain specific projects may have other elements of interest, or there could be subsets or elaborations of these elements. But invariably, all of the above seven will be in your company's system development process, whether you are a one-man start-up or Intergalactic Business Megalith and Sons, Inc.

To be ready to seriously fund a project, all interested parties need to agree that the details of those core elements have been brought up to a certain level of completion, fullness, or readiness. So the high-leverage question of this chapter is, simply: "where are we now?"

The results of that probe will be:

- finding out where your team is with regard to completion of those elements, and

- finding out any gaps in completion that need to be filled.

Let's look at each of the seven core elements one at a time.

OPPORTUNITY

As a starting point, every project will have a core element known as the "opportunity." It's the rationale for the project. A business opportunity has six stages it can move through. They are:

- *situation identified* -- a situation exists that could be addressed by a software-based solution, likely having at least one stakeholder who is willing to make an investment for better understanding of the potential value and possibly some allied stakeholders,

- *solution identified* -- the need for a software-based solution has been confirmed along with likely stakeholder needs, a formal statement of the problem with its root causes is available along with at least one proposed software-based solution,

- *value established* -- the business value of a successful solution has been established along with an understanding the various impacts on the stakeholders of that solution and the system's value as contribution to the business solution is established,

- *solution viable* -- a solution has been outlined in appropriate documentation with indications that it can be developed and deployed within company constraints and manageable risk,

- *solution addressed* -- a usable running solution that effectively addresses the opportunity in a satisfying way which the stakeholders agree is worth deploying, and

- *benefit accrued* -- the operational use of the system creates tangible benefits with a return on investment at least as good as anticipated.

Clearly, the last two items do not apply when you are at the beginning of a project; when you are trying to fund it. Thus, the more qualified query for you to ask the team is: "Which of the first four stages most apply to where we are right now?"

Then, you all need to decide which of those first four stages is the most appropriate as the point to fund substantial money. Most likely the discussion will center on stages three and four as the ideal place to be for funding purposes. In this particular discussion it matters less whether you choose three or four. It matters more that the choice you've made together is a consensual one. Be alert to any gap that may exist between where funding is ideal and where you actually are. Be prepared to open the dialogue further to resolve those gaps.

During that dialogue, many of the words used might need refinement in order to avoid arm waving and rambling. For example, in *solution addressed*, what are the criteria for determining "satisfying?" Or in *benefit accrued*, how, exactly, is return on investment going to be measured? Some homework is necessary on your part, and possibly the team's part, to go over the above stages prior to the dialogue to fill in some of that detail for discussion purposes. Be forgiving if your team has not been in the habit of defining these vague words. This kind of exploratory discussion, typically not done in the past, is what solidifies a project's good start.

STAKEHOLDERS

Now let's look at "stakeholders." The stakeholder core element can move through six levels of engagement. They are:

- *recognized* -- the stakeholders have been identified along with agreement about which subset of all of them is to represent the group along with the responsibilities of those representatives,

- *represented* -- the representatives have been formally appointed, authorized, are willing to take on their responsibilities and to use an agreed-upon collaboration tool or mechanism while integrating with the team's way of working,

- *involved* -- representatives carry out responsibilities, provide feedback and make decisions, in a timely way, as they communicate progress promptly to the stakeholder group,

- *in agreement* -- stakeholder representatives agree that their input is valued and respected by the team, agree on priorities in collaboration with the team and have agreed on minimal expectations for deployment,

- *satisfied* for deployment -- representatives have provided feedback on the system behavior as viewed from their stakeholder group perspective with confirmation that the system is ready for deployment, and

- *satisfied in use* -- stakeholders are using the software system, providing feedback and confirm that the system has met or exceeded the minimal stakeholder expectations.

Much like "opportunity," the question for you to ask for funding purposes is: "Where are we with regard to the first four levels of stakeholder engagement?" Many people find that the second level is adequate for funding purposes, but lust for a level three or four situation, optimistically hoping that the engagement will increase over time all by itself. It won't. But you can improve it by working at it using some of the material in the later chapters.

The engagement level choice here depends on system scope, complexity, and newness to the organization of any proposed project technology. Larger, more complex, highly innovative or exploratory systems could need a solid level four. If the system looks like it has a very long development cycle compared to typical prior projects, level four engagement is crucial.

REQUIREMENTS

The "requirements" core element has six levels of completion. But as we'll see, it does not necessarily have an absolute best level of completion with regard to funding. Also, its level of completion does not need to identically match the level of stakeholders or any other core element. For example, if stakeholders are at engagement level two (*involved*), requirements need not necessarily be at requirements number level two (*bounded*). The levels of requirements completion are:

- *conceived* -- the opportunity and need for a new system is obvious with the kinds of system users identified and some initial funding sponsors identified,

- *bounded* -- the purpose and extent of the system solution are agreed with well-defined criteria for success, appropriate mechanisms for documenting requirements including marketplace or internal assumptions and company constraints,

- *coherent* -- the helicopter view of the project is clear and shared by stakeholders and team alike, with relevant usage scenarios explained, priorities established, requirement conflicts noted and addressed, together with an understanding of the impact to the company,

- *acceptable* -- stakeholders agree that the requirements describe an acceptable system having good value, that ongoing volatility of the requirements is controllably low, and the portion of the opportunity satisfied by the requirements being obvious,

- *addressed* -- there are enough requirements to describe an acceptable system and they accurately describe what the system does and does not do so that it is obvious the system is worth making operational, and

- *fulfilled* -- the system fully satisfies the requirements and stakeholder needs with no outstanding requirements preventing completion of the project.

When you ask the question "where are we with regard to completion of requirements", you will learn a great deal about how well-formed is the solution to the business opportunity. There are several useful answers depending on the nature of the proposed system. Generally, you could consider *bounded* as the minimum you should accept for funding purposes. *Bounded* does not mean or imply that the system specifications are "frozen" and can no longer evolve. The sense here is that scope of function is known and the boundaries or edges with other systems are clear.

However, certain software systems could be so exploratory in nature, using such new or untried hardware technology or user interface designs, or even worse, have enormous political implications for failure, that "*conceived*" is all you can get as an answer from your team. In that instance, you probably only want to fund a pilot project -- something you are willing to throw away in order to learn about the gray areas of your understanding of what would be satisfying in the long run. Retrospective evaluation of that pilot will then allow development of a more *bounded* set of requirements. Start-ups can often find a pilot project useful in this way.

For non-exploratory or routine systems, having at least *coherent* requirements is important. *Coherent* takes *bounded* a step further to insure that initially conflicting requirements are resolved and both team and stakeholders understand the system utility and impact the same way. That shared understanding preempts later finger pointing. It minimizes additional recovery funding that could be necessary if dark, murky or difficult corners of the requirements emerge.

When the probable cost of the system is perceived as quite high relative to company norms, *acceptable* is likely the best option. Demanding that level of completion forces the team to think about the volatility of the entire environment in which the system is being built. It forces the team to acknowledge how changes in the environment might influence final system satisfaction -- things like marketplace desires, government regulations, uncertain hardware availability or performance, erratic availability of quality team members. This early focus on environment volatility will subtly, or maybe not so subtly, influence the attention team members give to ideas like fittings between system components and architectural flexibility that we talked about in earlier chapters.

If you really want to nail this environment volatility aspect down, you could ask the team for a formally written document, let's call it the Volatility Extrapolation Document, which elucidates all the things that could change and how the system can handle or can be easily adapted to those changes. Such a volatility document has not traditionally been considered a part of "requirements." But we highly recommend it. See Chapter 8, the VoxDoc, for details.

If the proposed system is making you feel exceptionally queasy in the stomach for reasons which are hard to articulate, then, to be conservative, requirements should be at the *addressed* level of completion. (The *fulfilled* level is the day you celebrate with, hopefully, champagne and rave reviews.)

There is one last point about requirements. In the incremental approach that we talked about earlier, it is not necessarily true that all the requirements for the completed system need to be developed to fullness all at once before beginning any construction of programmer code. Requirements may be developed in clumps that are applicable to each iteration in that case. Thus, the stages of requirements completeness mentioned above might apply one at a time to each clump, or for the first few clumps, rather than the entire system at once. For a project constructed iteratively, common sense also indicates that there should, however, be some thoughtful, top-level architectural documentation that is at least in the stage of *coherent* so that the iterations have a common guidance as they are built out. And none of this is permission to write code "playing it by ear" on a continuing basis.

SOFTWARE SYSTEM

In the bad old days, people used to inquire "how much of the software is done." The answer, historically, was invariably "the programming code is 95% done, sir." The 'doneness' of the system would hover around that number for weeks or months, with no visible increase in stakeholder-requested operational features. In these good new days, the answer has slightly retrogressed. We still hear the same number, but the meaning of 95%, as useless as that metric is, has been confounded by a multiplicity in the industry of different methodological approaches to constructing software, different software "schools," different ways of working, for a team.

Methodological approaches that teams use to construct software, using labeling nomenclature like Agile, Scrum, Kanban, SAFe, DAD and so on, each have different conceptions and different work products that contribute to what the phrase "95%" might mean. Because of the jargon differences in these approaches, it can be an exceedingly frustrating task to actually get a feel for what's going on across multiple teams when each team uses different ways of working. As a top-level executive trying to understand "where we are now," you can ameliorate this frustration by thinking of system doneness in a way that bypasses the jargon. Rather than looking at number of lines of code, we look at instead qualifiers about actual operating capability.

There are six jargon-free levels of software system doneness, they are:

- *architecture selected* -- the team agrees on criteria for selecting an architecture that addresses key technical, marketplace and political risks along with the hardware platforms, technologies and programming languages to be used. Buy versus build decisions have been made and opportunities for generalization and extended return have been agreed upon,

- *demonstrable* -- enough key architectural char-acteristics have been demonstrated as working so that relevant stakeholders agree the architecture is appropriate. Those key characteristics exercise critical or high risk technical and/or political interfaces in such a way that any important options in system configuration have been tested,

- *usable* -- the system can actually be operated by users who experience in operation the desired quality characteristics, features and performance according to agreed-upon test criteria. Current bug levels are acceptable and the likely to be delivered feature set is known,

- *ready* -- stakeholder representatives accept the system with its current user documentation and stakeholder representatives actually want to make the system operational (Whew, that was close! Let's have a party.),

- *operational* -- at least one system instance runs in its target environment and is available to intended users within the target service level agreement availability time frame, and

- *retired* -- the system is either no longer supported or updates will no longer be produced or the system has been replaced and/or discontinued.

Clearly, at the funding point in the calendar, the doneness of a yet-to-be-produced system cannot be considered *retired*. The likely appropriate answer for the "where are we now" question is the first level of doneness, namely, *architecture selected*. But a word of warning here. If the system contains a great deal of technical or political risk, or is being made by a group of teams that are geographically and/or linguistically separated, or it is a "pilot project," you might want to fund just enough money to get to the level of *demonstrable*. When everybody can kick the tires of a demo system and stop shaking when they think about the uncertainties involved, then you can then revisit the funding question for a finished system

Remember our comments from the previous chapters about generalization, extended return, and system tuning or optimization. Those activities typically permeate the *usable* and *ready* levels of doneness. When you are asking the "where are we now" question for funding purposes, you're likely not at those levels yet. Nevertheless, don't forget to include funding resources for those aspects. The *operational* level is the best place to allocate money funded for the review activity – discerning what can be learned about how well the software development process progressed for that system.

TEAM

Although they understand it intuitively and plan for it intuitively, it is rare that executives can articulate how they know when a software team is good, complete and properly assembled. Software teams have a kind of organic growth that ebbs and flows as the project advances because different skills are needed at different points in the system's evolution. Thus, a team is not necessarily fully and properly assembled just because it has reached the maximum number of people initially allocated. There are five possibilities for the question "where are we now" with regard to the team. They are:

- *seeded* -- for a mission that is understood by all involved, the required competencies and team size are determined along with an understanding of how to pace the ebb and flow in the growth of the team

- *formed* -- team has enough resources to start the project with team organization and individual responsibilities understood and sufficient competency to perform the work required,

- *collaborating* -- team members communicate in an open and honest way, working together as one unit focused on the team mission, and placing team success largely ahead of personal objectives,

- *performing* -- the team works efficiently and effectively, adapting to changing context while producing high quality output with minimal backtracking and rework and setting aside appropriate time to identify waste and eliminate it, and

- *adjourned* -- the team is no longer accountable usually because responsibilities have been handed over to support facilities thus freeing up team members for new assignments.

There should be no surprises to you in these team qualifiers. If you're actually talking to the team in your office, they are at least "formed" but not necessarily to the maximum number. However, to answer some of the questions of earlier chapters of this book, the team will have to be working together long enough to develop the background necessary to answer those questions. In fact, some of the discussions about architecture will require that they will have to have been at least *collaborating*. On a side note, for start-ups, it is possible and

OK that a person is both serving a role as stakeholder and team member.

Can you directly ask the team the question "where are we now" with regard to team status? It's a bit delicate, isn't it? A more approachable way is to ask the team to rate themselves, making sure they understand the rating scale beforehand. If your intuitive sense is that their rating is somewhat optimistic, you might want to bump the funding amount up -- but for a surprising reason.

What's the reason? In a private conversation several years ago with Capers Jones, that master of all things precisely measurable about software productivity, I asked Capers, "Okay, off the record, C. J., what's the best way to tell that a software project is really humming along like gangbusters?" Capers looks at me, pauses, chuckles and then says, "the bar bill." He then added, "This is especially important if the team is composed of people who are widely separated within the company either organizationally, politically or geographically." On that note, we leave it to you to work out the next best move for a non-collaborating team.

WORK

The day-to-day status of the team's efforts can be characterized in six ways. They are:

- *initiated* -- the person who gives the go-signal is known along with any constraints, management sponsorship strength has been thought out, the funding model is clear, and important project priorities are understood,

- *prepared* -- cost and level of effort is estimated, funding and other necessary resources are available to start, management policies, procedures, system acceptance criteria and dependencies are defined and agreed, risk exposure is understood including overrun or emergency funding,

- *started* -- development work has been broken down into actionable items which are actually started and are being monitored using clear definitions of the meaning of "done" for that item,

- *under control* -- work items are going well and completed within estimates, measurements are in place to show item progress and velocity of construction, risks are controlled along with unplanned work and rework, estimates are revised as necessary,

- *concluded* -- work to produce results is finished with the possible exception of housekeeping activities and the stakeholders have accepted the system, and

- *closed* -- all housekeeping tasks are completed and officially closed, backups of everything have been made, lessons learned and metrics have been made available for public review and comment.

Note that there is no notion that one of these levels might be something like "95% done." However, there is an explicit demand for some kind of measurement and monitoring of tasks and development artifacts. Most people would opt for work status level two, *prepared*, as necessary to begin funding discussions. In subsequent chapters we discuss various ways to strengthen management sponsorship of the project if there is a gap preventing a rating of the work status as *prepared*.

WAY OF WORKING

In the bad old days, most people didn't give much thought to the formal concept of a team's "way of working." It was just "the way things were done around here." However, carefully-tailored ways of working -- the tools and day-to-day procedures used -- can reduce waste, risk, duplicate work and unexpected software programming effort that seems to spring up unbidden from the fan dust of the programmer's computer. Thus, as a top-level executive, it is worth your time to probe this aspect of things to some extent even though the ways of working themselves are likely not familiar to you in any detail. There are six status levels that a well-conceived way of working can have. They are:

- *principles established* -- industry acceptable software development principles are selected and committed to, along with agreement about necessary supporting tools and practices that fit the understood context the team operates in,

- *foundation established* -- the key important practices and tools are available and any remaining gaps in them are analyzed and understood, gaps corrected where possible, thereby enabling integration into the team's day-to-day routine,

- *in use* -- at least some members of the team are using the way of working with regular discussions about successful use while the rest of the team begins adapting and supporting the way of working based on feedback,

- *in place* -- all members have access to the practice and tools and use them, adapting the way of working as a result of regular inspection and discussion of what's going well,

- *working well* -- team members spontaneously apply the practices and tools without question, making progress as planned and experience the natural support of the way of working, and

- *retired* -- the specific way of working used to construct their system is no longer in use, but the lessons learned are shared for use in future systems.

Unless you are really technically savvy, the innards of a way of working will sound as intelligible as poorly spoken Etruscan. You don't need to understand the innards though, in order to know "where we are now." Most executives find that level two is the ideal funding point. The detail you most need to be alert to is this: are there gaps in the needed tools and practices? For the purposes of funding, level two should be in place because getting to that level frequently requires that some resources, like training or money, are allocated to fill in gaps so that the team can get started moving towards level three. The team will have identified what is required to do their mission. You need to know if a gap exists so that you can to be sure those gap-filling costs are identified and included with sufficient lead time to acquire them.

We have finished the questions of this chapter, giving you a jargon-free way of monitoring the software construction process at the front end. But before we move on, we would like to make a big hat tip. The counsel of this chapter is an executive-level adaptation of an industry standard called Essence, a standard of the Object Management Group that you can find at http://www.omg.org. It was originally developed by SEMAT at www.semat.org with important input from the Ivar Jacobson International Company. Because you are an executive, we have deleted the computer-heavy lingo of that standard (purists will undoubtedly weep, wail and post flame messages on Facebook, Twitter and Amazon) so you can use those insights bolstered by your own creativity and management savvy to go forward. We also added a few generally useful pointers about software development here and there, pointers based on our experience with a few thousand software developers and managers over the years. Your friendly neighborhood software guru will be your loyal ecstatic slave if you ask him to explain some of the subtleties, nuances, other uses and historical development of the Essence standard that are not covered here.

This chapter has described the last of the series of steps that you use to extend your influence over the value returned by your software project. The management-by-query style we have discussed extends your power and influence by leveraging certain timing points in the calendar while at the same time accounting for inherent characteristics of software building. With them, you implicitly intervene for positive benefit without requiring extraordinary technical knowledge on your part. These questions give your team a subtle message, namely, things are going to be different.

How does that happen?

It happens because you expressed interest and authority in areas that they have not likely heard you speak about before. They will follow your lead. However, depending on the maturity of the software development side of your company, these ideas and interventions could seem quite radical or controversial to the team. Or they could be mistaken for just another management fad, soon hopefully to go the way of all the previous management exhortations.

Wouldn't that be a waste, right?

In the next chapter, then, we will talk about step 12 which prevents that waste.

Step 12 details the techniques of "insertion" or transition of these ideas into your company -- techniques to make sure these ideas don't become just another exhortation having no lasting results. We'll explore how to time the use of your power to get a company to effectively, smoothly and maximally absorb the ideas of extended return, architectural flexibility, incremental delivery, and Essence concepts when those ideas are foreign to your team's way of thinking.

POINTS TO PONDER

Think about a project in the past which was unhappy for you and/or stakeholders or otherwise was unsatisfactory. What would have been useful questions that should have been asked at the "inception power point," the beginning of the project? What stopped those questions from being asked?

During the most recent software development process in which you were involved, what are some of the other points in time when it would have been magnificently, spectacularly, wonderful beyond compare, if you could have known, with some precision, how far along the project had progressed?

Does your company have teams who have religious arguments about "methodologies" or other ways of working? If so, can you place a dollar value on how much time could be saved if these arguments went away, because everyone had a common vocabulary to monitor progress despite different ways of working?

What stops one of your teams from learning improved software development techniques that have been discovered by another team? What resources would be needed to fix this transmission of expertise? What would be evidence that inter–team transmission of expertise was flowing?

PART 2 – MAKING SUCCESS HAPPEN

5

Assessing Your Team's Anarchy

Since this is a book about timing, you might find yourself asking the question "When should I take action with the ideas of steps 1 through 11?" Let's call that collection of ideas -- architectural evaluations, incremental approaches, and the jargon-free vocabulary for monitoring progress and so on -- "Good Stuff."

If you are managing a software group that is part of a start-up company, that group likely has not yet developed any bad habits. Their software development history is perhaps not longer than a few months. A few months are not enough time for developers to get attached to their way of working. Change will be easy. So the right time is now. Do it. Ask those Good Stuff questions.

On the other hand, if you are interacting with a more seasoned team, one having a long history of software development, say, 2, 3, 10 or more years of history building software, the software development habits will be very ingrained. Before you use the ideas of this book to influence the success of projects with that type of team, it is important to time that use so that your team grows into the ideas in a complementary and synergistic way. The remainder of this book is step 12. This step shows you how to time and organize that growth.

In environments with a long history of software development, it is tempting to hope that company management could simply issue a directive to use Good Stuff and it would all be done. However, just as the questions of those first 4 chapters have a most appropriate time to be used; your initial use of these ideas in that seasoned context also has a most appropriate time. If timed inappropriately, your team's ability to respond can be drained by an unexpected phenomenon. If that drain occurs, your new influence will get short circuited.

What's the explanation of how this drain can occur? Earlier, we talked about the idea that system components have fittings or interfaces to each other or their environment. Good Stuff, it turns out, may be thought of as a component in the much larger picture of a company's overall processes. Similar to a computer component, Good Stuff has central functional principles and it has an interface: the connection between its principles and your team. And just as we suggested that you can ask questions about a technical component's interfaces, you can ask questions about the interface between Good Stuff and your company. From the helicopter view, the overall management by query question is: what is the match between the interface of Good Stuff and the way your people work now? Is the interaction between Good Stuff ideas and your company likely to be simple or complex?

If there is a mismatch between the interface of Good Stuff and your company, results will be slow or will not reach management expectations in proportion to the amount of the mismatch. If the amount of mismatch is large enough, a complete failure to absorb Good Stuff could occur.

Good Stuff has an interface that most easily fits into a company that has a low level of "anarchy." Anarchy may seem like a strong word and perhaps it is. However, almost every company has some parts of its software development process which, if revealed, would make embarrassing headlines in the International Herald Tribune. For any given company, when the sum total of all these embarrassing spots passes a certain threshold, anarchy can be said to be more present than order and discipline. If the amount of anarchy exceeds a certain critical mass, Good Stuff concepts can't take hold. In fact, they will fail. People will point fingers at the failure, probably blaming Good Stuff concepts when other factors having to do with the internal disorder are really responsible.

Before you use Good Stuff, would you like to know a way to find out in advance how much anarchy is currently in your company? That way, you could then predict the likelihood of success. If the likelihood presents more risk than you would like to take, you can apply the appropriate resources, resources which we will explain later, to mitigate that risk.

The first task is to measure anarchy with a test, a test which, as you now might predict, is made up of questions. You answer the questions, score the answers and draw conclusions. We provide some commentary on some of the various ways in which other people from other companies have scored. You can cheat, of course, and skip over the questionnaire to the commentary. Such cheating optimizes your time at the expense of the fresh insight that comes out of taking the test before knowing the answers. Whether or not you choose to cheat is part of the test.

There are two different perspectives from which you could approach the questions:

- answer the questions using your own personal perspective or

- answer the questions by imagining the response of someone below you in your company, a person who will be directly affected by the evolution to Good Stuff (called an "evolvee" in the questionnaire).

For the moment, we suggest you answer from your own perspective even if the question might be better answered by someone working at a different level from you. You may even have to guess because your own personal experience does not include enough context from which to make an informed answer.

That's OK. Take that guess and note to yourself that you need information about what's going on from evolvees in your company concerning that question. Later however, it will be very revealing of your company's character to have several people take this test, some from upper management and some at the developer level. The scores should then be compared. Often these different staff levels have wildly different views on some of the questions. Those differences also represent a certain kind of anarchy. The differences should not the ignored; they need attention in proportion to their impact before Good Stuff is propagated.

TAKE TEST NOW

(See <u>Appendix 2</u> for Test Questions)

Did you cheat? Did you skip to here without taking the test? If you detected that there were two questions which had the number 5, we know you took the test. And because of that you also get to reduce your score by one full point because your thinking processes are clearly quite sharp and that will give you a positive head start on any anarchy that exists in your company.

HAVE YOU GOT THE ENERGY?

Sir Isaac Newton, famous for falling apples, observed that a physical body, once it starts to move, tends to continue in that original direction until a new force is applied. Installing Good Stuff follows similar principles. Good Stuff represents a new direction; thus a new force must be applied to get a company moving in that direction. In a way, this test measures how much force needs to be applied. If the average score is high, great energy must be applied. Notwithstanding how proud you are of your team's drive and punch, companies only have just so much energy to throw around. If all or most of the company energy is being dissipated by dealing with problems in the anarchy category, there will be very little available for moving in the new direction. This test measures the likelihood of success when moving to Good Stuff if no new energy is added to the company.

An average score in the range of 6 to 10 are "danger" scores. They indicate that it's time to get your resume mailed off to the nearest corporate recruiter. If you are the owner of the company, start looking for a buyer - as the importance of software continues to intensify; competitors with lower scores are going to eat your lunch. Scores in the 6+ range indicate that the available resources for change of anything in the company, whether it is Good Stuff or the repainting of water coolers, are quite low. Therefore, the probability of success is low. Put another way, there is a lot of work to be done before your team is fit enough to begin installing all of Good Stuff concepts successfully.

If you had an average score in the range of 1 to 3 – well, probably you're reading this book so that you can gloat to yourself about how great it is to work in your company. In fact, maybe you should close this book and hand it to the executive sitting next to you in the airplane because that person likely needs it more than you.

Scores in the 1-3 range are rare; perhaps one percent of all people who have taken this test report this kind of score. This score means either that you downplayed your team's problems, or your team has things so well in control that implementing Good Stuff will not be impeded by extraneous distractions, or the team doesn't need Good Stuff at all.

Most likely, your score is in the range of 3 to 6. We call these values "challenge" scores. If you make no preliminary repairs to improve team fitness, introducing Good Stuff will be a distinct challenge. The effort will get easily derailed by issues unrelated to Good Stuff. Let's look at the logic behind that possibility.

HOW YOU COMPARE WITH OTHER COMPANIES

This test has been given, in introductory software management seminars, to representatives from about 400 companies of various sizes and market sectors. The composite team score of those representatives was about 6.5. But the score for individual questions, especially those individual questions with scores greater than about 6, is much more interesting.

Let's examine the nature of the composite team represented by all the answers the respondents gave to the questions. That implied software development composite team is quite interesting in its patterns and conflicts. Analysis of this composite team will provide some useful insights that will help explain why a mere strongly worded edict mandating Good Stuff would fail to cure the inadequacies of the team's way of working.

To arrive at the composite score, we took a simple arithmetic mean of all responses. This average is not an ideal statistical tool for these purposes, so from time to time we will comment below about how the values were distributed around that average.

ONLY FOR MASOCHISTS

The composite team picture is a bit dismal. Here is the description of that team, as indicated by the high scoring questions which are referenced in parentheses. This team is staffed by people in a constant state of high overload (Q4) and managed by managers who want code yesterday rather than maintainable code (Q5). Very little bug prevention, such as walkthrough meetings where code is publicly reviewed, is used (Q7) and little historical data is kept to trace the source of bugs (Q9). User specifications are informal (written on coffee lids and backs of hamburger wrappers) (Q12).

In this team there is little understanding of the generally accepted software design principles of coupling and cohesion (Q16- see Glossary for definition of coupling and cohesion). Team priorities emphasize "tight code" at the start of the project rather than a later budgeted, managed approach to system optimization (Q17). As an aside, "tight code" means system code that has been optimized for speed or other possible optimization choices. Naming standards are not emphasized (Q15). During the budgeting for projects, managers "negotiate" the time estimates derived by developers to a shorter duration (Q18). Few formal development processes are in place (Q19) and practically no metrics are available to monitor post-delivery software maintenance costs. Of the questionnaire's 21 questions, this composite team hasn't even a single question that scored 3 or lower.

This environment of the composite team is a truly hopeless hell, and the mere installation of some strongly hyped developer tool into this environment will have as much effect as talking even louder to your cell phone when the battery is dead. The team is locked in a cycle of self- defeating practices, which would likely spoil any software technique and render that technique powerless. There is no way this team will ever have a Good Stuff success; it is doomed to suck on Chaos.

Strong words, you say. Let's follow the logic of it all.

HOW A TEAM GETS IN ITS OWN WAY

This composite team has no development process aspect in the 1 to 3 range. This suggests in general, that everything is a problem -- not surprising since respondents said they were in overload. When everything is a problem, no team energy is available to accommodate the change to Good Stuff concepts because all available energy is being absorbed by crises occurring everywhere else.

A team needs to have some sense of surplus resources in order to absorb the training and familiarization processes for

Good Stuff and the other ideas your new power question approach introduces. Even with a sense of surplus resources, a Racko rule of thumb is that a company can only absorb 2 ± 1 significant cultural changes at a time. If the team staff is in overload, insufficient time will be given to learning Good Stuff concepts and the implied common vocabulary. This leads to wheel spinning argument about team progress. The distraction short changes the system code quality. That leads to dissatisfaction with Good Stuff and thus it either fails or fails slowly.

We could really stop here and from this alone surmise that the road to successful Good Stuff implementation will be a hard one. This team's doom is sealed by the specifics of the other process flaws which have high scores. The managers appear not to want maintainable software. They want on-time delivery instead, so they can be expected to covertly or overtly sabotage efforts by developers to take time to learn or apply the Good Stuff concepts.

So we can expect system code components will be produced in a random way because no formal prioritization process exists. The system code components will be named whimsically (without easily remembered, consistent names) because no naming standards are in place. The system code components will be buggy because walkthroughs will not generally have been done.

A team has many choices for the organization of the architecture -- only a few of them are good. Because the managers "negotiated" shorter time estimates, the architecture will not get the iteration and rework needed to make it truly useful and generalized. Those good choices need to be looked for and discovered; they do not spring fully formed into the developer's head.

If a developer does sneak in some extra undocumented overtime to refine the architecture, not much progress will be made because the tight code will resist rework. The badly designed, hard to remember architecture will contain few business components that have extended return, because the user specification process is so primitive that such components didn't get discovered.

The small amount of extended return which might have squeezed through this formidable set of barriers will go undetected. Why? Because no metrics exist for making meaningful comparison of a system built using Good Stuff with earlier legacy systems.

No feedback process exists in this whole sorrowful sequence to trace bugs back to their source. Thus anything learned while fixing the badly designed, buggy system code components will not be used to improve the overall software development process.

We end up with bad system components having marginal extended return, no way to measure that return, and no feedback mechanism to help correct any of this.

Even if a company started a Good Stuff installation effort, what company would continue with Good Stuff if this was the final outcome? The only manager who would put up with this state of affairs as the launching pad for Good Stuff is someone whose hidden agenda is to keep Good Stuff from happening. If you have followed the logic above, it should be obvious that no amount of classroom training budget, development tool dollars, or head scratching over which vendor offers the best Good Stuff training will effectively change this team's possibilities.

ONE BRIGHT SPOT

The composite team question (Q14) having the lowest score (3.4) attempted to determine if source code version control disciplines were used. "Version control" is the formal recording and archiving of artifacts of every step in the construction of a system component. This archiving enables rolling back to an earlier version of a code component if a later version develops a hitherto unseen bug.

Scores in the survey sample for this question clustered around 1, 2, or 3. These scores are really quite good. It means that should any good system components ever happen in this company, say around Christmas time, then it would be easy to find the original programmer's code when enhancements are to be made.

The profile of the composite team is a useful tool to gauge the probability of success in Good Stuff for your company. To time the insertion of Good Stuff correctly, every place where your team matches the low scores of the composite profile is a place to change before you get too far into Good Stuff concepts. Then you can begin to ask the questions of chapters 1 through 4. If you are already deep into Good Stuff installation, strong, immediate efforts to alter any of your team's inadequacies which match the poor scores will help ensure your success.

If your own profile is not as dismal but nevertheless there are some high scores, attend to those first. Appendix 3 details the risks and potential consequences of ignoring high scoring questions.

The next chapter details how to time the reviving actions when a team has a worst-case or closely similar profile.

POINTS TO PONDER

Does your company have a way of measuring employee overload? Is the concept of "employee burn-out" a concept which is not politically correct to talk about?

Do you know how much undocumented overtime is likely occurring? Does your company rely on undocumented overtime, but nobody talks about that fact?

Is there a formal post-delivery software process review mechanism in place? Is it working? How do you know? If not, what stops this from happening? What resources would be needed to improve it?

6

Dissolving Team Anarchy

After you've evaluated your company's state of anarchy, the next task in timing the insertion of Good Stuff is to decide how much remedial action to take regarding your team's anarchy level. If your anarchy score is low, or if you only had a few high-scoring questions, you might skip to the next chapter.

Since statistics favor that your team does follow the high anarchy profile, in this chapter we'll suggest what you need to do to get your company out of this mess. Then you will be able to install all of Good Stuff concepts successfully. If you were going to enter a rider into the multi-kilometer Tour de France bicycle race, you need to first make sure the rider is fit. Fitness is established from some baseline or track record. The high-anarchy profile we have in the composite team is not a fit one.

Here is the good news: it is possible to form an orderly attack on a worrisome composite team profile. A large amount of pure legwork is involved that anybody could do in the early phases. The bad news: you won't like it. It is very hard. Very unpalatable. A lot like eating sand and walnut shells together. Only certain people are ready for that. If you have read this far, it's a good bet you can do it. Also in using the word "you" we can't know for sure whether you are the CEO reading this or a stalwart knight appointed by him to clean up the mess. This section is written more for the perspective of that knight but a top executive should understand how it all plays out.

Let's quickly review the high-anarchy profile.

This "average" team is staffed by people in a constant state of high overload and managed by managers who want any kind of code at all by yesterday rather than easily maintainable code possibly delivered later. Very little bug prevention, such as walkthroughs, is used and little historical data is kept to trace the source of bugs. User specifications are informal. There is little understanding of the generally accepted software architectural design principles of coupling and cohesion (see Glossary for definition). There is an emphasis on "tight code" (also called "efficient code", see Glossary) from the start of the project. Component naming standards are not emphasized. During the budgeting for projects, managers "negotiate," trying to shorten the time estimates derived by developers. Few formal development processes are in place, and practically no metrics are available to monitor current software maintenance costs or identify instances of extended return.

This particular profile has two important parts to it - the big picture and the little picture. In the big picture, there is the software department working as a service to some larger company goals. In the little picture within the software department, there is the individual software process inadequacies mentioned above. The company goals of the big picture are the context which, in the long term, fertilizes the growth and maturation of the software department in the little picture.

The state of utter chaos described by the high-anarchy profile suggests to us that the correction of that little picture chaos is not currently viewed by highest levels of management as having any significant benefit to the big picture company goals. As long as that is true, attempts to move towards Good Stuff concepts by correcting the individual process inadequacies in the little picture will be thwarted by lack of upper management support. Therefore, the first thing to do is to find out why upper management tolerates this mess.

There could be many reasons for this tolerance. Here are some.

It could be that the software department does not currently provide anything of real bottom line utility to upper levels. For example, the software department might only have charter for employee payroll, plant layout, parking lot assignment and medical insurance. Important things, to be sure, but not things where the software development process improvements would directly affect bottom line profits. In this situation, upper management levels will not routinely give software much priority or budget for improvement.

Another possible reason is that upper management could be ignorant of the effect of bad software practices. This would be true if, for example, the costs of maintaining existing software versus the cost of new software were hidden in a lump sum budgeting process.

The next step, then, would be to find out the reasons. Once those reasons are discovered, the next thing is to present a convincing case to the appropriate management levels about why improved software development can dramatically impact the bottom line. In detail, that means bottom-line improvements from such things as increasing revenue, avoiding costs, improving customer service, improving inter-office political distractions or possibly obeying external regulations.

Notice that we did not say to present a case showing how Good Stuff concepts improve the bottom line. There is not enough fitness yet to say that, let alone deliver such improvement. Timing is important here. We will talk about building a rationale for Good Stuff in the next chapter. If it is not possible to build a dramatic case for the utility of improved software process without naming Good Stuff concepts, go home, play with the kids. For the high-anarchy team profile, upper management must be turned around regarding general software improvement or all is lost.

When management is convinced, first start examining exactly what is the cause of the "overload" which everybody seems to be feeling. Unless the overload is reduced first, there will be no energy available in the day for anybody to absorb and accommodate the changes that are going to be put in place next. It is easy to get cynical about overload and presume that all people will say that they are overloaded irrespective of their actual state. But even if that is a realistic appraisal, probing for the details of that perception will reveal some highly useful data.

The high-anarchy team profile has four likely sources of overload:

LITTLE PICTURE OVERLOAD- within the team:

a) overload generated by the inefficiencies inherent in the chaos itself,

b) overload caused by too many concurrent technology changes being attempted simultaneously.

BIG PICTURE OVERLOAD- the team as a service to the company:

c) overload generated by interfacing activities required to coordinate with other departments,

d) overload caused by continuing system rework that is the typical result of an informal system specification or architectural design process.

REDUCE OVERLOAD BEFORE STARTING

Form a small team to ask everybody to try to identify the overload source. Find out whether the overload source is from events in the little picture, source (a) or (b), or the bigger picture (c) or (d). If it's a big picture source, go back to upper management (who is now on your side because you presented a dramatic bottom line case earlier) and make some suggestions that will reduce the overload. At the risk of being obvious, it's useful to remember that during this presentation you will be talking to non-technical people who may not be cognizant of concepts like "software process." Therefore, find graceful ways to describe what you would like to do in terms that are more likely to be in the vocabulary of upper management, for example, "market directed team optimization." Often, upper management will grasp (and therefore approve) your goal faster when the descriptions are market-oriented or otherwise familiar and bottom-line related, rather than software process jargon related.

If the source of overload is from the little picture (a), inefficiencies caused by the internal chaos, don't worry about it. That kind of overload will diminish of its own accord once process improvement starts really happening. If the source is too many concurrent technology changes (b), that's a tougher challenge.

As we mentioned, a company can only absorb just so many significant changes at a time, perhaps as few as two. So the choice is to fail (or more likely delay) either accomplishing the technology changes or the software improvement changes. Present this particular choice to upper management in a most careful way and go with what they decide. If the choice is to go with many changes simultaneously, prepare to fail slowly at all of them.

For overload coming from the big picture, (c) or (d), wait until overload has died down in response to the suggested optimizations which upper management sanctioned. Once overload from all sources has been reduced, you can begin laying the foundation for fitness.

BUILD CONSENSUS ON FOUNDATION CONCEPTS

Next we want to handle remedial action on all the high-scoring anarchy questions in a particular order. Do not train about Good Stuff concepts details yet. First, build the foundation. Schedule training classes on walkthroughs, basic system design, architectural concepts of coupling and cohesion, and the benefits of software process review. Then all the developers should get together and hash out the initial standards to be used to give orderly names to system components. These particular standards will be better adhered to if as many people as possible contribute to them.

In reality, all of this training is not about education, per se. It is really about building a common vocabulary for the way of working within the little picture: common but specific definitions for frequently overused words. At the risk of boring the more informed reader, this team profile needs common agreement on the meaning of basic words. Here are some typical ones:

- "maintenance" Does it include work done on new code added after delivery of the system to the user? Bug fixes? Customer feature enhancement requests? Code that should have developed but there wasn't time before delivery?

- "good software" Does that mean fast? Tight? Efficient? Usable? Having extended return? Understandable? Friendly? Easy to modify? Easy to read by a new team member? Zero defects? And crucially important - get consensus about which adjective gets priority when a time crunch occurs.

- "design" Does that include reworking the design during development to make it better (without adding new code), or is design just a one shot thing done at the beginning?

- "walkthrough" Is the benefit from the interaction and communication at the meeting? the bugs found? the traceability?

Consensus agreement about these words will also help improve communications with upper management in later steps, as well as reduce overload coming from source (c) interdepartmental coordination.

Once people have the common words to view the factors which contribute to making "good software," people in the team can begin to talk about what might be useful to measure and trace in the software construction process. Tie what is measured to things which could immediately aid the upper management marketing goals that were discovered earlier.

For example, you might decide that establishing a way to trace where in the construction process bugs arise is more important to upper management's market goals than measuring the costs of fixing bugs. This could happen if your company is a high-profit software vendor with customers who always buy the upgrades. A different kind of company might decide both are important.

It almost doesn't matter how you decide this one. You can always change your mind. What's important is the open discussion and implementation, using a common vocabulary, of this self monitoring of software development process. The ability to professionally monitor the efficacy of the software development process is a hallmark of being fit.

Put in place whatever you have decided to measure. Then wait (timing, again) to build up some statistical base. When the base is built, celebrate by announcing that everyone is now ready to become certified Good Stuff concepts users.

We've charted a timing sequence which will make a dead team walk again. This sequence will test your patience, but it will get your team fit to tackle Good Stuff concepts and get benefits delivered. Consider outside consultant help to organize some of the details. In any case, remember that avoiding remedial action on a team with a high-anarchy profile will simply cause Good Stuff concepts to fail slowly.

In the next chapter we will discuss how to build support for Good Stuff.

THE SECTION BELOW IS FOR DEVELOPERS ONLY - NO EXECUTIVES OR MANAGERS ALLOWED IN THIS SECTION

A specific software development process flaw, the one in which managers shorten developers' estimates; can be dealt with at any time in the above list of remedial actions. The best time is to start early. However, it can proceed as a parallel effort to the strictly sequential steps outlined elsewhere in this chapter. The fix does not require any management approval or budget and can be done only by developers. Well, maybe not only by developers, but we assume that most managers who do shorten estimates either don't recognize how dysfunctional that practice is, don't feel they have the freedom to change the practice, or are out of ideas. So here is the quick way a developer can bust this practice by using questions to covertly retrain that manager.

First of all, as a developer, never quote one absolute number for the time period for the estimate. A one-number estimate is an irresistible temptation to the dysfunctional manager to shorten that estimate. Prepare a range of estimates, say three, covering worst case, best case, and most likely case. Have a closely reasoned justification why the worst case estimate might occur. Importantly, the developer must say what would have to be true for the best case number to apply.

Break out a separate estimate for "integration." Be able to explain that integration means effectively testing all the assumptions people have made about the connections between modules or system components -- an activity most managers seem to think takes no work. "Effective", as used here, means that other members of the team or other related groups can verify that their code has the right hooks so they can fit your code into theirs. It also means verifying connections to databases, local client/server networks, the "cloud," and other external but interacting systems. Typically, it also includes documenting the system components which are deemed potential candidates for redeployment with extended return in future systems. This written material is a mandatory piece required for any future systems that will integrate themselves with the redeployable code. Without this documentation, extended return cannot happen.

The developer tactic is to present an obviously thoughtful estimate which has many parts and pieces so that a routine and perfunctory request to make it smaller can be countered by politely asking which part or piece the manager would like to omit. A hard core estimate shortening manager might say "I don't want to omit any. Make them all smaller." The honest response is something like "Do we agree that integration is composed of organizing a system component and its interface so that it works for the other developers, connecting to the databases through the network, and documenting components so that we can get the benefits of extended return where possible? Are you asking me to shorten the time for those things? Do you want me to tell the other developers that they can't use the component because only half the integration hooks are tested? Or tell the sales department that we can't connect to the databases because only half a connection is there?" We could call this series of developer questions covert "management-by-query" done by the developer, even though in this instance, it's the developer managing the manager.

If upper levels of management have sanctioned software improvement in general, the dysfunctional manager will soon learn that he can't omit or shorten integration, that some things simply are not elastic. And as the manager discovers from your estimating style what it means to be a successful Good-Stuff-concepts-oriented team, the role of whipping boy will be a thing of the past.

7

Enhancing Your Power by Exercising It

In the previous chapter we spoke about tactics for success that were needed if your team's environment was a state of anarchy. In this chapter, we will be precise about what leadership aspects are appropriate for you when *inserting* Good Stuff after all the anarchy aspects have been taken care of. In a modest way fitting a book of this size, we would like to give a little more precision to how your insertion leadership is best expressed. In most companies of any size, after all the anarchy is removed, *the way you time and demonstrate that insertion leadership* is the single most important factor for success.

Got that?

Three people writing software out of a garage loft for a start-up will decide to adopt Good Stuff concepts over cold beers one night without any special leadership. That will be the end of discussion and the beginning of sustained success for that small business. A global firm with 3,000 people in its information technology department won't be able to even find a beer hall large enough to hold such a meeting, let alone successfully conclude it.

Some kind of a sustaining force is needed to hold the adopting company on course during the time of the adoption period.

Many people expect that the obvious advantages of the easy to understand jargon-free vocabulary and architectural focus of Good Stuff concepts are sufficient to inspire all the top management levels. However, unless the advantages can be tied to something meaningful to all management levels, most of the people who are within your sphere of influence will not be grabbed by those advantages.

The key to insertion success is new ways to implement that sustaining force. We'll call this sustaining force a "power cascade." The major ingredient in sustaining that power cascade is a compelling rationale for installing Good Stuff. You need this more than just the initial head nods from other levels of management. The goal of a power cascade is to unleash a cascade of action, over time, from every level involved in this insertion of Good Stuff.

You may have already had some thoughts about this rationale from reading the previous chapters. In this chapter we develop the rationale and add to it the "everything else" refinements beyond the timing concepts of earlier chapters.

We believe the Good Stuff concepts rationale should have three parts, each targeted towards a different segment of the company in order to tie as many people as possible into this cascade.

RATIONALE - PART 1 – INTERNAL BENEFITS

For the first part of that tie-in, figure out why you want to use these concepts in terms of internal company software processes. What software process improvement do you want to get from installing Good Stuff concepts we have covered? Is it--

1. More precision and agreement about where a project stands in its time line, especially if there are multiple teams?

2. Better communication between stakeholders and the team?

3. Ability to understand progress across multiple teams using different ways of working?

4. A focus on extended return and redeployment of components across a family of systems?

5. Easy maintainability of delivered code?

6. Flexibility of your finished system?

7. Improved coding productivity?

8. Lower Training Costs?

9. Other?

The results of the questionnaire of Appendix 2, taken from a sample of managers and developers, may also provide guidance about useful choices from this list.

For most people, assigning a priority to those choices and making a selection will be easy. Let's pick one and say that you are going to Good Stuff concepts because you want better communication between stakeholders and teams. Great. Once you have picked a choice, here is the very important question - what stopped you from getting that choice in the past? Good communication or any one of the other goals of flexibility, maintainability, and productivity, is something most companies have always wanted. So what got in the way in the past? Unless that can be explained in convincing detail, you haven't a chance of getting it now.

Since good communication is a most popular reason to switch to Good Stuff concepts, it's valuable to explore some of the things that have prevented it in the past. We believe that many companies don't have good communication because they actively inhibit learning from past systems and the subsequent process improvement that would result. Consider the following conversation we overheard in a company that prides itself in its slick, excellent communication. It was between a low-level manager (MGR.) and a developer directly under him (DEV.).

DEV.: From our experiences on the Digital Umbrella project, we can clearly see that we now have a solid collection of system components which would be valuable to other people in the future.

MGR.: Let's go out to lounge. (Takes DEV. out to lounge, serves him coffee.) It's Blue Mountain Special. I made it myself this morning. You know, I think you are the unofficial VIP of the team and anything you say I take very seriously indeed.

DEV.: Thanks. I thought these components would be helpful to the company.

MGR.: Before we look at these components, let me invite you to think like a manager for a moment and let's look at the bigger picture, in confidence, of course. We all want to finish on the already agreed upon date, don't we?

DEV.: Well, yeah. Of course, I do.

MGR.: You make very important contributions to the company. You can be especially proud of this extended return idea.

DEV.: Well, shouldn't we do it more?

MGR.: Isn't it too risky? We don't know if we will get any payback, don't you think? I'm sure that looking at it from this top down perspective you can see that, too. You can do that can't you? Even if it means putting your suggestion off till a later date? I will try to find budget to give you a crack at this at a later time. I feel good about the way this outcome balances goals. Now that I have put this all together for you, are there any other things that need to be talked about?

A manipulation, unspoken but firm, is happening. The manipulation that is covertly employed by MGR. is to absolutely prevent the discussion of his real priority, the schedule. He covers over that manipulation by sugar-coating it with routine slather about "contributions." There is not professional, candid communication here. In fact, it is a kind of evil "management by query." There are mixed messages which superficially espouse empowerment and positive attitude but effectively preserve unilateral control by the low-level manager. A long-term result of repeated interactions of this kind is that DEV will stop taking any kind of initiatives that improve the software development process. Installing Good Stuff concepts under these circumstances will be met with cynicism and will eventually fail.

Breaking this manager to developer game is fantastically difficult for most companies. They rely instead on appealing but useless (under these circumstances) measures like purchasing some software package which the selling vendor says will boost productivity. Before that measure could ever succeed, the company needs to find a way to look at the unspoken, un-discussable goals like maintaining schedule or maintaining unilateral control.

Especially if the schedule is being met by heroic pro-gramming described in earlier chapters, the company needs to examine carefully the question of exactly how much unpaid overtime is in its long term interests. How has heroic programming prevented improved productivity, system architectural flexibility, extended return and maintainability in the past? The company should also examine what prevents open discussion of the un-discussable. With those answers, a process-based reason for Good Stuff concepts can be developed that has substance and utility. The process-based reason for going to Good Stuff concepts should then be published as one sentence such as "We are going to Good Stuff concepts as a first attempt to break the strangle hold on quality caused by our previous emphasis on scheduling as opposed to quality communication."

Could you do such a thing?

It takes phenomenal courage, unshakable determination and balanced humility on the part of everybody to come up with a sentence as forthright as the quote above. Your desire to have this sentence says all those same qualities about you. You may find that outside consultants are very useful during this endeavor to keep everyone on track. Contact http://www.timingisalmosteverything.com/helpme for ways to get started.

RATIONALE - PART 2 - THE MARKETPLACE

The second piece of the rationale doesn't require soul-searching. It is another reason for moving to Good Stuff concepts but one which has an external, marketplace oriented basis.

For example, suppose that the marketplace was requiring very frequent product releases or upgrades. Then, the company might wish to emphasize extended return because time to market is becoming increasingly critical. Of course, there would also have to be the thoughtfully researched basis to believe that there is substantial extended return potential among new market product releases or internal business practices that hadn't been tapped before. There must be some formal evidence that a family of related products or services exists. After all, merely wishing for extended return won't make it happen if products are too dissimilar. Or as another example, a company might wish to focus the Good Stuff architectural emphasis in order to prioritize flexibility over extended return because the marketplace for products was composed of users who were very changeable in their needs.

Whatever the marketplace-oriented reason, it should be packaged into a simple sentence that everybody at all levels can understand - "We are going to Good Stuff concepts because it will help with the East Europe distribution problem" - "We are going to Good Stuff concepts because our products are a family; our software is a family" or some such one-liner. The details of the way Good Stuff concepts implement these statements may involve coding productivity gains or flexibility or maintainability or whatever. That detail needs to be spelled out somewhere so that any developer or manager can know the game plan and the sequence of plays. However, that detail need not be in the one liner sentence.

RATIONALE - PART 3 - A DEVELOPER WIN

The third piece of the rationale is an internal, company-oriented piece. However, it is a piece that focuses on and appeals to the developers of the new system. It is a reason for going to Good Stuff concepts which has a direct payoff to the developers in some way they highly value. As an example, consider this sentence - "We are going to Good Stuff concepts because Ms. Big, the boss, knows that those concepts are the best boost to everybody's career path that is available at this time." Ms. Big, of course, needs to be frequently heard saying this at 50,000 watts broadcast volume from time to time. The idea behind this piece of the rationale is to give a personal incentive to developers that need retreading in order to encourage them to absorb and use Good Stuff.

Your power cascade is strengthened when lower management also has a personal win from the shift to Good Stuff concepts. And the three-part rationale is designed to provide the basis for those lower management level wins in the first two parts.

How? The part of the rationale that deals with the marketplace is important to all good managers. If the details of how Good Stuff concepts will improve marketplace posture are convincing, fair, un-hyped, and real with things like return on investment spelled out, then a rational low or mid-level manager should respond positively.

A rational manager will also respond surprisingly well to the first part of the Good Stuff adoption rationale, the part that deals with what was previously un-discussable. It will be a breath of fresh air that inspires new energy. When this effect reaches a critical mass in the culture under your attack, the drive to adapt Good Stuff concepts becomes self motivating.

POWER CASCADE BOOSTERS

You can add even more rocket fuel if you can find the individual hot buttons that key managers have. Usually, these hot buttons are hidden. They are not part of any manager's formal job description or part of any overall corporate strategy. But they are nevertheless very high-priority goals in the near-term for the manager.

Typically, such hot buttons are idiosyncratic. For example, some managers might have a current morale problem in their team, others might need to bring in a project within a certain error rate, and still others might need to reduce budget for outside consultants, etc. Your task is to find ways, however remote, that Good Stuff concepts might be useful is resolving some of these more individual, hidden goals.

Example: "Burt, you are absolutely right about the need to watch the consultant budget. However, the right Good Stuff consultant, who would agree to a bonus for an on time system deployment, which you, Burt, would be good at setting, will end up costing us less overall. The consultant would work on using Good Stuff to promote improving communication between stakeholders and users thus speeding delivery of the total system. The consultant's acceptance of such a bonus deal would also give us a sanity check on our sense of schedule." To the extent that the move to Good Stuff concepts address some of the hidden goals of key managers, that is the extent to which key managers really feel your power cascade efforts.

There you have it, the key actions to sustaining that initial edge. All of the other things in earlier chapters are important - learning the architectural and business value questions, setting the funding point intelligently, examining and fixing the anarchy issues, possibly starting with an appropriate pilot project, appropriate training and so on. Success is dependent on the well-thought-out execution of all the component parts involved in such an important move. But a journey begins with its first step, and, crafting a strong power cascade is the most important one.

HOW TO TEST YOUR POWER CASCADE QUALITY

Everyone assumes that a leader is leading when he simply signs the check for whatever new improvement goody is being proposed. In fact, a mere check signer will likely elicit cynicism from developers if the check signing has no follow through in the other activities that support the goal of the approved goody. Below is a list of things power cascade aware executives think about and do every day. These are 4 dynamic characteristics of power cascade aware executives who are committed to maximum influence - ways they show the world that they really want the benefits of Good Stuff concepts:

1. They "work the crowd" like good politicians, talking up the Good Stuff both among peers and developers. They do this over the long term.

2. They acknowledge people who help make the shift to Good Stuff concepts by creative rewards of some kind. If people make multiple contributions along the way, the manager (and/or check signer leader) makes timely cumulative rewards along the way as well.

3. They require periodic progress reports about Good Stuff concepts, goals, and usage from all subordinate management levels.

4. They find ways to involve all subordinate levels of management in the pursuit of Good Stuff concepts goals, not just the lowest developer team captains.

The last characteristic is exceedingly significant. People so often think of a power cascade as emanating from and ending with a single (top) person.

Not true!

A power cascade must permeate forcefully from the top down with obvious follow through by managers in between the developers and the top. Otherwise, the drive to Good Stuff concepts will get lost in a black hole of middle management (see next chapter for more about this point). In other words, each level of management must have their own way of daily expressing the above 4 dynamic characteristics.

One final note – For any manager involved in the Good Stuff transition, the presence or absence of these 4 ways of behaving is a good test of the quality of your three-part rationale for Good Stuff concepts. If managers seem reluctant to do these 4 behaviors, that indicates that the 3-part rationale needs more refinement and punch.

POINTS TO PONDER

What is a possible one-sentence internal reason to adopt Good Stuff?

What is a possible one-sentence market place oriented reason to adopt Good Stuff?

What is a possible one-sentence developer win-oriented reason to adopt Good Stuff?

If you managed a successful insertion of some corporate change in the past, how many of the 4 dynamic characteristics of a power cascade did you use?

8

Putting It All Together – Tips and Tricks

In the previous 4 chapters of this 12th step, we examined things that need to be done to insert Good Stuff into your company. In this last chapter, we will refine some options and finesse tactics about timing and sequencing those options for new projects. Also, we will cover projects that have already begun, but which you nevertheless would like to influence in a positive way.

There are many ways to think about introducing the concepts of this book. You undoubtedly have someone who can plan a major roll out of a new technology or software concept. This chapter will not attempt to substitute for all the detail that person might employ. But the roll out of Good Stuff involves your personal power and thus there are some pieces which would not ordinarily be a part of a company's usual roll out approach. There are some turns and choices to be made, as well, depending on individual circumstances as we show below.

START HERE

If there is currently a computer project underway whose progress you are following, you could just begin by asking the 10 high-payback questions of Chapter 2 and 3 to your technical staff. Before you launch yourself in that direction, we'd strongly recommend that you look over the Glossary and Appendix 1 - "Improvisations on the 10 High Payback Questions." There is no need to memorize the explanations or question variations. But familiarity will add to your presence.

You might also decide to apply the concepts of Chapter 4 and attempt to figure out approximately where that partially started project sits on its own time line. Your staff may not have a Software Floor Plan Diagram or equivalent handy for the system you want to probe. But, such diagrams are not that hard to prepare. Technical staff does not need elaborate training to learn about this from currently available technical books. All of this means you can get the questions answered fairly quickly.

Getting more preferable answers to your questions over the long term, getting Good Stuff concepts as a permanent fixture of your company, with the attendant advantages of monitoring progress with precision - these goals are more complicated. Let's review the macro-steps necessary for that, in order of their occurrence in time.

THE SURVEY

The questionnaire of Appendix 2 should be used to help get a reading of your developers' view of the world. If your developer group is bigger than about 50, start with a small group. Do everything intelligent to get honest answers, rather than a whitewash of current problems. Inspect whether scheduling or other matters are un-discussable topics. If the anarchy scores are genuinely awful, slow down and fix up the most glaring deficiencies before going on.

It is tempting sometimes to treat high scoring questions casually, presuming that developers are "just grousing" or are otherwise unappreciative or unmoved by management efforts you consider significant. Be sure to consult Appendix 3 regarding those high scoring questions whose results you might tend to dismiss out of hand. Listed there are the risks you expose yourself to if, in fact, the developers' high score questions are a realistic appraisal of the situation in your company. Compare those risks with the risk of losing the power you are trying to enhance because the software staff perceives management as blind to reality, and then make the appropriate choice.

CALCULATING THE PAYOFF

Suppose you believe that the common vocabulary of Good Stuff concepts will foster extended return across a family of related software projects, thus making it a high priority reason for bringing in Good Stuff concepts. You should have some technical staff run the numbers and look at the actual dollar payoff.

Form a Reconnaissance Team to evaluate the dollar payoff from your chosen goal. In the case of extended return, their task is to scout around for commonalities like: (a) a family of products that appear to form the basis for some core components, (b) some common business practices across divisions or departments, or (c) common customer types.

The team should be composed of at least some members who are from other divisions or multiple product areas. Why? Because otherwise, later acceptance of results by the other divisions can be difficult even though the discovery team does good work. A team from a major international money center bank found more than a third of all 100+ business procedures were shared across a half dozen or so business lines, a remarkably good team discovery and the start of a fine collection of core components. The team wrote gorgeous documentation. But initial acceptance from the various business lines was light because there was no support for people from those business lines to participate in the original discovery team.

An extended return reconnaissance effort can be easily overdone with teams spending years to develop an eight-inch-thick, twenty-pound document containing all the possibilities. Set a time limit- something shorter, say nine months or less. See what they find. Other Good Stuff payoff goal types will typically have shorter reconnaissance times.

Make sure reconnaissance team members work the numbers. In the enthusiasm for the payoff, it is easy to be misled about costs. Here are three commonly overlooked costs for the extended return payoff:

- cost of your best people,

- cost of zero defect quality assurance, and

- cost of generalization of components.

Why these particular costs? Your best people should be on the task of designing and producing the extended return components. Otherwise, the future users of the components will ignore the components because they will suspect that the components are not well thought out, easy to understand and easy to use. An unyielding quality assurance approach to the components is necessary because none of the future users of the components will pay attention if they have the slightest doubt about the stability of the components. Finally, there is a cost associated with making sure a component can, in fact, fit into a multiplicity of systems; i.e., the cost of generalizing the component. Generalization can often add as much as 50% to the base cost of an otherwise working component. Thus, the cost consideration to acquire extended return is not insignificant.

After you add in support costs (the cost of warehousing the components, distributing them, advertising them, maintaining updates to them etc.), you may also find that the components don't start paying for themselves until they have been deployed in as many as 8 new systems. Such a ratio is not unusual. Some people get discouraged by that ratio, especially if they can't identify that many new future systems which may use the components.

However, even without promising future system utility, having re-deployable components can have other advantages. For example, suppose your company is suddenly faced with the inexorable approach of compliance with some Federal regulation and many programs to certify as having compliant behavior. The generalized components could save several weeks across different testing runs in the certification process. When there are unyielding deadlines, the time savings can be important even though the components will not necessarily be needed again in future systems.

DEVELOP THE 3-PART RATIONALE

Once the payoffs are known, and the data from the survey is in hand, the three part rationale can be formulated and broadcast around the company. Do not underestimate the cleverness needed to coax middle management into excitement about your move to Good Stuff concepts. Middle management people are often worriers who easily can get stalled by a preoccupation with budgetary concerns. If you start your power cascade broadcast there, it will get derailed by the concerns that perennially occupy the middle levels. Instead, start the broadcast with the lowest level technical staff and build some grass roots support for Good Stuff concepts first. Generally, the technical staff will embrace the rationale easily because you designed it to intentionally have some obvious wins for them.

Then, after the technicians have gotten excited, present your Good Stuff concepts goals to middle-level management. When the middle levels experience the simultaneity of grass roots support plus the top management heat, even the most inertia prone will go along as that action simply appears to be the safest course given the pressures from above and below. Middle-level managers need to be included in any Good Stuff concepts roll out reward scheme as well.

All non-technical managers affected by the change to Good Stuff concepts should get tuned into the sense and vocabulary of the 10 questions of Chapter 2 and 3. From time to time, use the tests suggested in Chapter 7 to evaluate the ongoing quality of your power cascade and the rationale's continuing effectiveness.

Often there are key supporters, managers who are relied upon to keep up the momentum. Develop a backup plan for replacing the drive of these key supporters, should the whims of Fate cause these managers to be transferred for some unrelated reason. One feature of a backup plan is to make sure something useful and good happens early due to the adoption of Good Stuff concepts -- ideally not greater than nine months after the transition start. The delivery of something useful within a short period will engender new support from people who were once only casually interested.

THE FIRST PROJECT

Once anarchy has been eliminated as a factor, and the Good Stuff adoption 3-part rationale is constructed, pick the first project on which to try out these concepts to see how the communication ideas work out. The ideal project is a low-risk one. A lowest risk project is typically one that is a rewrite of an existing software system. The advantage of using an existing piece of software as a first project is that if anything truly unexpected happens, there's always the old piece of software to fall back on.

Life isn't always this easy. Instead you may have a business crisis – you need find a way to get some product out the door or cease a particular line kind of business altogether - a very high-risk situation, indeed. If you have to choose a project in circumstances like this, take extra care to make sure your lead architect and lead stakeholder representatives are thoroughly trained and comfortable with Good Stuff concepts or bring in an Good Stuff concepts consultant.

Of course, schedule appropriate training for the other people on this first project. However, be aware that training does not turn a developer into an Good Stuff concepts supporter. The rationales do that.

After the team is staffed and trained, the team will take a little while to refine the business problem statement and then derive a suitable architecture for the computer solution. The architecture should be ready for your 10 high-payback questions at approximately the ¼ point in the estimated project calendar time.

It is also possible that portions of the architecture may be ready either earlier or later than the incremental building plan the team developed. In which case, it may be necessary to ask some of the questions a few times rather just once.

FINESSE

There are certain things you can add to the above efforts, which are refinements. When you use them, you underline the seriousness of your intent, thus reinforcing the enhancement of your influence early in the project whee it counts.

The first of these is in the area of rewards. The literature abounds with reward schemes - rewards for the creators of the Good Stuff concept roll out program, rewards for the utilizers of Good Stuff concepts, rewards for the supporters and managers, rewards for the team vs. the individual. And did we leave out debate over what actually is the most effective kind of reward? Deciding exactly which of these schemes is right for your company is beyond the scope of this book. However, here are some finesse ideas regarding rewards.

This book is about enhancing your power by modulating when you exercise it. Let's look at rewards timing - the way in which rewards for Good Stuff supportive actions are made. To start with, it is important to establish early that the rewards, whatever and however you decide them to be, are not an entitlement routinely dispensed by rote from the Personnel Department. Instead, they ideally should be something which only a top executive could really have the power to bestow, something which obviously is the prerogative of only the top echelon, something, therefore, that in its very bestowing reinforces the implied power of the bestower.

An example of such a reward might be a free monetary draw, up to some limit, against an otherwise unaudited expense account. That draw is allowed to be used for any purpose and any mix of purposes - funding a research project, enabling a neighborhood social project, buying experimental high tech gear, going on vacation, hiring a specialist consultant or whatever. Another example is that of a special title, not on the usual career ladder, which has out of the ordinary privileges or powers. Awards of this nature need not necessarily be announced publicly, and in certain ways have more force because they are given one-on-one by the top executive. A complete reward program might usefully be a mix of such "silent" awards and public ones.

It is common to think that reward opportunities exist only for the employment of Good Stuff concepts within some specific project. But much more can be gained if you:

- give rewards (early in the roll out) to people who encourage the move to Good Stuff concepts (e.g. a developer who spontaneously helps a new hire learn Good Stuff concepts), and

- give cumulative rewards -- multiple contributions to the transition effort earns multiple rewards (e.g. the same developer next shows the sales staff how to use the Software Floor Plan Diagram and Good Stuff progress monitoring ideas to close a sale of some software product that you offer to the public).

When you give early rewards to people who help encourage the transition and spread of Good Stuff concepts, you multiply your own effectiveness to make the company change happen by rewarding people for being exponents of the transition rather than just utilizers. When you give cumulative rewards, especially if you make them quickly after each contribution effort, you let people know that your interest is undiminished over time and that lots of glory is available. These two together start to generate a self-perpetuating transition.

THE VOXDOC

A second finesse point is the use of a symbol which always reminds people of the seriousness of your intent to be on top of the significant issues for projects. Many people think of such symbols as posters, slogans, desktop medallions and the like. But you need something more active, something that involves the developers daily.

We suggest a new document, one that we briefly referred to in the earlier chapters when we were discussing adaptability to change. It is called the VoxDoc.

The VoxDoc (Volatility Extrapolation Document) is a document which is not part of typical development methodologies. It has value during the entire development process. Its idea is a simple one:

- capture the significant technical problems of previous systems,

- capture the design solutions to those problems,

- extrapolate or speculate, from those solutions and current business trends, the ways in which the project of interest is liable to change, i.e., liable to be volatile,

- produce all components with reference to these learnings and insights, and

- designate a responsible individual, who at every stage in which a new component is designed or integrated, officially signs off that component as having been reviewed against the learnings in this document.

The VoxDoc is prepared in the very early stages of system construction, as pointed out in Chapter 4, by people with software analysis and design skills. For all later stages of system development, it becomes the official reminder: a major business value of the system is an architecture which can adapt to change and preserves useful expertise of past systems. In addition, the VoxDoc is a vehicle which establishes a practice common to other engineering disciplines: the practice of traceability. Should a component prove troublesome, not easily redeployed, vulnerable to impact from environmental changes or otherwise unsatisfactory, the component's history and parties concerned are available for tracing and corrective review. The combination of these purposes keeps the team focusing sharply on Good Stuff.

PLAN FOR SUCCESS

When the Good Stuff concepts take hold, a surprising number of unintended, but wonderful, consequences can happen. It's worthwhile to speculate to yourself, based on your understanding of your own company context, what might in fact occur. Less infighting? Fewer Stakeholder complaints because communication was enhanced? Fewer surprises about delays? Resilience in the face of changing specifications or marketplace needs? Savings because of extended return?

Lay out in your mind the way you are going to let people know you are happy with those wonderful surprises. Have those ways ready for the right time to celebrate.

RedHat, in its adoption of the material of Chapter 4 (Essence ideas) was pleased to discover the upper management surprise and delight about the new consistency the use of Essence enabled across internal project processes. Hewlett-Packard, in their instrument division, found potential to profitably redeploy significant software across a family of 16 products.

May the gods of Good Stuff smile as favorably on you.

9

Conclusion

Two hundred years ago in America, prairie houses weren't generally built using floor plans. People cut down trees, roughly finished the wood and put together the house with a few craftsmen. It took time for house building to mature into a formal, more error-free process. Now, however, it would be bizarre to build houses without a prior architectural conception, a subsequent series of detailed blueprints and floor plans, along with a formal building process with predictable risks and ways to measure progress. One wonders, therefore, why it is not considered bizarre when complex software projects are still run in ways that befit primitive times.

This can all change when you enhance the helmsmanship that is properly yours.

And why not? The 12 steps of this book give you all you need:

- a set of non-geek questions you can ask your technical staff that will help deliver better business value from your software systems; questions which will surprise and enliven those who report you,

- critical tactical timing guidance that gives you the best leverage for communicating, adopting and transitioning your staff to the Good Stuff ideas behind these questions,

- jargon-free monitoring tools about software system progress which you likely have never had before,

- an objective way to diagnose the trouble areas in your software development process and ways to positively affect them, and

- insights into what has previously inhibited the smooth exercise of your power in the information technology arena.

Are you going to make things different?

Imagine, in your mind's eye, that it is a year from now. You are looking back at the successful ways you implemented some or all of these ideas. Customers are ecstatic. Support issues are way down. Your people are talking to each other in a new way. As you look back, what else is different? Which things went more smoothly? What did you see that was a pleasant surprise? When did you first see a change in the way the team members interacted? What makes the new systems seem more solid?

And now, right now, on a scale of 1 to 10, where 10 is the passionate desire of a teenager for his first car (or horse, or space ship as the case may be), how much do you want that success?

POINT TO PONDER, but only after you answered the prior question.

Why did you not give a lower rating to that prior question?

ONE FINAL NOTE:

Before you go, I'd like to say "thank you" for purchasing my 12 step guide. I know you could have picked from dozens of books on software management. But your intuition led you to my approach. So a big thanks for purchasing this book and reading all the way to the end.

If you like what you've read, then I need your help. Please take a moment to leave a review for this book on Amazon. This feedback will help me continue to write the kind of books that help you get the business results you want.

When you decide you need outside resources to enhance project success in the form of:

- one on one executive coaching on the ideas of this book,

- class room group training on adoption and insertion techniques of this book's Part 2 section,

- speaking engagements,

- diagnostic help in pinpointing team challenges,

- audio books and CD's elaborating selected book contents,

- tailoring the ideas of this book to unique project contexts,

then go to TimingIsAlmostEverything.com/helpme to arrange a one on one discussion of currently available success assistance.

Appendix 1
Improvisations on the 10 High Payback Questions

In seminars and executive coaching sessions, people have asked if there is more than one way to ask the first high-payback questions of steps 1 through 10. Some people didn't want to appear as if they were reading out of the book. Others simply wanted variety, since they knew they would be asking them many times. Still, others were concerned that they would make up a variation that would lose something in translation.

Here are some things to remember. The questions are important to phrase usefully, but the final tests are: did you get an answer, can you understand it and are you satisfied with the answer. If you ask a friend, "Shall we go to dinner tomorrow?" and the answer is "My car is in the shop" – you got an answer but not to the question you asked.

Perhaps the car's state is influencing the choice, perhaps the person doesn't want to say yes or no at this moment. This kind of off-topic response is easily mistaken for an answer, and in casual conversation many people might simply infer a negative answer from that response. But the answer given is not an answer to the question. Inferring is not the same as understanding. The answer is a diversion and should be probed further unless politics or tact clearly indicates restraint will temporarily serve better.

At the risk of boring readers who are already clever conversationalists, we do caution against asking variations to the questions that begin with or contain the word "why" as in "why do we depend on fiber optics?" Questions with "why" tend to elicit justification or beliefs rather than objective data and thus are not as helpful in solidifying business results.

Preferable questions would be "what stops us from using something else besides fiber optics?" or "what is the benefit from depending exclusively on fiber optics?" or "when did we decide to rely exclusively on fiber optics?"

Note that each variation also takes the conversation into slightly different directions.

The 10 questions are shown first in their original form as stated in the main text. Next follows a review of the general objective of the question – what is it probing for. Following that are the improvisations.

Some improvisations are more direct, some less direct. Variations of one question may slightly overlap those of another question. Some variations are not even questions but are statements. However, when said with a rising voice inflection, or alternatively, followed by a short pause, they will then have the same effect as an explicit question.

In any event, we'd like to you to relax a bit about this, have some fun with the variations and make up your own, rather than consider it some kind of performance test.

QUESTION #1 - What Goes On in Each Box?

Objective: Question #1 is a first probe for good design. If simple sentences cannot convey useful meaning about the components, the team doesn't have its arms around this application yet. This question lets the team know that you want to poke around inside this system, see how it is put together and that you will not be satisfied with a simple feature description like "it helps our employees understand our company benefits."

Variations:

- Give me a one sentence description of what goes on each box.

- I'm curious about the most important function of each box.

- I wonder if you could tell me what the most crucial activity in each box is.

- What's the business value delivered from each box?

- What's important to know about each box?

- Explain each of the box's job and how they work together.

QUESTION #2 - How much dependency do we have on X?

Objective: With this question you are evaluating the risk the new system will present to your business due to dependencies, and whether they are internal or external to your company, data or services. "X" is anything on the Software Floor Plan Diagram connected to another box by an arrow.

Variations:

- What kind of risk do we have regarding X?

- What is our backup if X goes down?

- I'm wondering if we have any significant risk because of our dependency on X.

- I'd be curious to know exactly what kind of business risk X gives us.

- Between boxes X and Y, which box most exposes us to loss of business? Of customer good will?

- How long does it take to recover if we lose the function of box X?

- Is X made by our people or do we rely on outside support or vendors?

- Is X the first of its kind for our team or do we have experience with it?

QUESTION #3 - Which dependencies have we chosen to insulate the system from, what factors led to those choices instead of others, and how have we done that?

Objective: This question probes the extent to which the system is insulated from the failure or unavailability of a dependency.

Variations:

- Is there anything stopping us from minimizing the risk of box Y? How can we better protect ourselves from a failure in box X?

- When did you decide to insulate box X instead of box Y?

- What thoughts prompted you to insulate box X but not box Y?

- How did you arrive at the priorities for picking places to insulate? What would it cost to insulate everything?

- Under what circumstance might box X become unavailable?

QUESTION #4 - What is the performance cost of the insulation?

Objective: The insulation will require some computer resources to do its insulating thus degrading to some degree overall system responsiveness. This question probes that impact.

Variations:

- How much will the system slow down because of the insulation for box X?

- What will the customers notice because of the insulation of box X?

- Do we run any performance degradation risk because of the insulation of box X?

- What would be the first thing the user would notice if we made the insulation of box X stronger? Weaker?

- Does this insulation hamper our ability to get faster systems next year?

- Do we process data slower in any way because of this insulation?

- Is our traffic capacity hindered in any way because of this insulation?

- I'm curious how we can have this insulation and yet seemingly not pay any penalty for it?

QUESTION #5 - Where do we insulate against changes in government regulations, competitive trends, marketplace trends, etc.?

Objective: This question probes for dependencies or assumptions which could be conceivably permeating all components, dependencies which are not related to the arrows, connections and interfaces in the Software Floor Plan Diagram.

Variations:

- What happens if the Department of Justice changes the rules?

- The local governments are considering (a tax on our activities, new legislation...) and I'm wondering how we'll handle that and in which box?

- Suppose competition offers a similar system, which boxes would we have to change to get back the edge?

- Which boxes are affected if we had to bring this system to a foreign country?

- Sales trends in country Y are unpredictable - which boxes would be affected either way?

- Customers are getting fussy about computer systems - which boxes give us the most leverage to respond to that fussiness?

QUESTION #6 - What happens if we change hardware or network components?

Objective: This question finds those components, if any, which have been specialized or adapted to particular hardware or network electronics. Such components typically have less flexibility for redeployment in future systems.

Variations:

- Which boxes contain proprietary components?

- Which boxes contain components that do not follow industry standards?

- What is the downside for (using, not using) industry standards in each box?

- Are the standards used in the system industry standards or are they rather what the major industry vendor offers?

- Can we replace the hardware with that of another vendor for less than X% of total cost?

- Are there any trends about network electronics that we could not adhere to?

- Where in the system has there been any attempt to get extra performance or speed by not following industry standards?

- Are there any network or vendor specific protocols which we are tied to?

QUESTION #7 - What happens if we add a new line of business such as Y?

Objective: This question probes the overall ability of the system to be easily reconfigured for a rather typical business tactic - adding a new business line. Beware of system architectures where the majority of components are affected by such a change. The likelihood is high that such an architecture has not yet been refined to the point where the real core of your company's business has been found.

Variations:

- Draw a circle around all the boxes affected if we merge company A into our operations.

- What could be done to minimize the number of boxes affected if we added product Z to the line?

- How many boxes would be unchanged if we took on product Z?

- What's the downside to the system if we add 5 new products?

- Which boxes are affected if we try to sell our current line in a foreign country?

- I'm wondering how the inclusion of a new market segment would affect the system.

QUESTION #8 - What happens if we want to share this system with another company or division?

Objective: This question probes for company life blood, the procedures that have utility across company boundaries, procedures representing accumulated expertise transmissible to the next generation of system developers.

Variations:

- What components can go into the standard library?

- Which boxes have the highest extended return potential?

- I'm curious how many boxes would be affected if we move this to another division.

- Which of those components can we put in inventory?

- Describe the level of effort required to redeploy each box in another system.

- I'm curious what we can pass on to next system.

- When would we know that we have gotten some additional return on our software investment from usage in other systems?

- What resources would be needed to package this system for use in another division?

QUESTION #9 - What are the system increments, in what order are we going to assemble them and what is the benefit of that particular order?

Objective: This questions explores the trade-offs (among market place risk, political risk, hardware risk and software risk) which were made and the criteria used to decide the order in which system pieces are assembled.

Variations:

- What trade-offs caused us to choose these system increments?

- What do we get by building the system parts in this particular order?

- Who gets the most benefit from the (first, second, third ...) increment?

- Which increment is the most (technically, politically, financially...) risky?

- When do we test the highest (software, hardware, network, political, financial...) risk?

- When do we test the lowest risk item?

- Which components get the most testing throughout all the increments?

- When does the user see functioning increments? (early is better)

- When does the user get to give feedback on the increments? (early is better)

QUESTION #10 - Is there anything stopping us from doing the integration and test/assessment on small increments rather than large?

Objective: This question is a direct cross-check on the size of each piece of the system to be assembled to determine if the size is optimal and planned or arrived at unconsciously. If there is something that is an impediment to making small increments, this question will bring that forth early in the project where effective resources can be applied. Generally, shorter time periods between increments (less than "months") is better although this is somewhat dependent on the level of user effort required to finish acceptance of each increment. It is also possible that some increments are not shown to the user but used only to validate internal technical issues.

Variations:

- What is the benefit of each size chosen for each of the increments?

- Is there anything preventing us from making smaller increments?

- I'm curious how we will control the bug location process during integration? (not the same as bug repair process or bug discovery process)

- What resources would be needed to do integration in smaller steps?

- Is our test plan fine grained or coarse grained? (use if your technical team employs the word "granularity" when talking about component size)

- What is the longest calendar time between any two successive increments? What is the shortest?

Appendix 2
Anarchy Questionnaire

The following questions reference something called "Good Stuff". "Good Stuff" for the purposes of this questionnaire means those parts of the architectural concepts, checklists and vocabulary of the first 4 chapters that are to be introduced into "the company." The phrase "the company" means the people in the group, division, department, team etc. who are evolving into developers, designers, managers, stakeholders who will be shifting to and using or are otherwise impacted by Good Stuff.

Each item below is about a topic in software engineering or an aspect of shifting to Good Stuff. Each item has a scale from 1 to 10. The sentence at the left of each item is the positive extreme of cooperation with, or interest in, the shift to Good Stuff. The leftmost sentence may also be thought of as the most disciplined aspect of that item's topic. The sentence at the right hand side is a worst-case statement of an aspect of anarchy or resistance or impediment to the shift. A "1" then, indicates that the item is not a problem or risk. A "10" indicates a significant or potentially significant problem or risk. Any given issue may, of course, be somewhere in between.

For each item, place a circle around the one number which represents your assessment of where the company (department, team etc.) best fits, either between or at the extreme. When answering assume the perspective of an "evolvee," that is, someone who will be required to learn about Good Stuff or who will be affected by the adoption of Good Stuff.

We invite you to feel free to be honest. Specifically, it will not be helpful to downplay real problems. The more accurately you describe your team and its environment now, the easier it will be later to correctly assess needed resources.

When you have finished answering all the questions, add up all the values and divide by 20 to get an average score.

For a downloadable PDF version of this questionnaire go to
TimingIsAlmostEverything.com/anarchyquestions

1. You believe that there will be rewards from the company in the form of something you truly value if you help accomplish making the shift towards Good Stuff.					You believe there will be no special rewards.				
1	2	3	4	5	6	7	8	9	10

2. Shifting to Good Stuff represents a good fit with the company's past values.					Good Stuff represents certain values that conflict with what most people at the company really believe and how they actually behave.				
1	2	3	4	5	6	7	8	9	10

3. You perceive strong political support for a shift to Good Stuff.					You perceive weak political support.				
1	2	3	4	5	6	7	8	9	10

4. I am not so burdened by current work load and pressures that it would be hard for me to assimilate the skills needed to make Good Stuff happen.					I am very burdened by other pressures and work load.				
1	2	3	4	5	6	7	8	9	10

5. I have been integrated into the load decision making process about projects.					Most of the decisions are still being made above me without much input from me.				
1	2	3	4	5	6	7	8	9	10

5. The boss asks us to give highest priority to making software that is easily maintainable.					The boss asks us to get software out the door Yesterday.				
1	2	3	4	5	6	7	8	9	10

6. We have a Usability Lab that gathers feedback from inexperienced users. Feedback gets factored rigorously into the product.					We use shorthand codes or message numbers to display errors. If it works, that's good enough.				
1	2	3	4	5	6	7	8	9	10

7. We prevent bugs by spending 10% of the development budget on walkthroughs.					We fix bugs by having a lot of unpaid and undocumented overtime.				
1	2	3	4	5	6	7	8	9	10

8. We have a department made up of journalism majors that write user documentation.					Developers write user documentation if they have time.				
1	2	3	4	5	6	7	8	9	10

9. When bugs are fixed, we rigorously log them and track them back to the development phase in which they occurred.					We just fix 'em.				
1	2	3	4	5	6	7	8	9	10

10. We routinely have a user on the development team.					Users won't talk to us or don't want to be bothered.				
1	2	3	4	5	6	7	8	9	10

11. We know the cost in dollar terms to repair a line of code. We have this data on a product by product basis.					We just fix 'em.				
1	2	3	4	5	6	7	8	9	10

12. Users present us with specifications that have industry standard diagrams or other formal notations which describe their needs.					Users hand us yellow sheets of paper with sketches and comments and hope we can decipher them.				
1	2	3	4	5	6	7	8	9	10

13. The team routinely uses CASE tools and thought before any code is written.					The team takes the yellow sheets and starts making screens and code from them right away. Hey, get real, coding is hard work, we don't have time for that CASE stuff!				
1	2	3	4	5	6	7	8	9	10

14. Old versions of code are routinely managed by a formal version control and library system.					Old versions of code are kept on USB flash drives somewhere, maybe on Charlie's desk.				
1	2	3	4	5	6	7	8	9	10

15. Code modules have part numbers.					Huh? We don't even have any naming conventions for modules or components.				
1	2	3	4	5	6	7	8	9	10

16. Everybody knows what cohesion in code is and frequently agrees on the level of cohesion a module has.					Nobody ever talks about it.				
1	2	3	4	5	6	7	8	9	10

17. We have a formal tuning and optimizing phase built into the development schedule where the system performance is tweaked.					We pride ourselves on being able to write tight code right from the beginning of the project.				
1	2	3	4	5	6	7	8	9	10

18. Upper management believes and respects my time and budget estimates.					Upper management always tries to renegotiate or shorten my estimates under any circumstances (or they have actually cut it recently).				
1	2	3	4	5	6	7	8	9	10

19. We regularly review our software development techniques, bug reports and costs to determine better ways to do things.					We do not even have a formal software development process that all projects follow.				
1	2	3	4	5	6	7	8	9	10

20. I have the authority and upper level support I need to get my work done					Upper management seems distant or uninterested in my problems.				
1	2	3	4	5	6	7	8	9	10

Appendix 3
Risks for High Scoring Anarchy Questions

Predicted Good Stuff Failure Modes for Individual Anarchy Questions

The interpretations below indicate the predicted effect of a high score for each of the Anarchy Probe questions of Appendix 2. In other words, this is what will happen if you have a high-scoring question yet say something like "this has been a problem for years, it hasn't seemed to have been all that troublesome, let's leave it alone."

It is not guaranteed that your company will experience these effects if there is management inaction concerning a high score. But common sense dictates that when you see a high average derived from many such questionnaires taken by many people in your company, you should be on the alert for the early warnings of the effects. The number prefix of each refers to the number of the respective Anarchy Probe Question in Appendix 2.

The interpretations that follow reference "Good Stuff" as a shorthand for both Good Stuff concepts, architectural and compatible management ideas that you might be putting in at "the company". The phrase "the company" means the people in the group, division, department, team etc. who are evolving into either Good Stuff users/stakeholders or Good Stuff developers.

For ease of reference, a synopsis of the high score statement of the questionnaire is presented in **bold** prior to the predicted risk for that high score.

1 - No special rewards for helping to make the shift to Good Stuff:

Initial supporters of Good Stuff will lose enthusiasm when difficulties of introduction happen and will, therefore, tend to abandon the effort. The population at large will cynically conclude that this is yet another management lip service goal which can be safely ignored.

2 - Good Stuff has certain values which conflict with established company beliefs and behaviors:

Any initial success will be discounted or played down. Management support will evaporate at the first sign of difficulty.

3 - Political support for Good Stuff is perceived as weak:

There will be no middle-level management support for the specific costs associated with generalizing usage of Good Stuff across all departments. The transition will fail slowly.

4 - Very burdened by pressures and other workload:

Continued confusion about development status and mismatched communication between users and developers because Good Stuff terminology skill levels will be low due to lack of training or insufficient time to absorb the ideas. Continued poor quality software components will lead to dissatisfaction with and, ultimately, blaming Good Stuff.

5(a) - Decisions are made from above without much input from below:

Scheduling conflicts will prevent adequate time for generalization of components especially with regard to the VoxDoc. Low understandability of the code and poor generalization will lead to low amount of utilization and thus low extended return.

5(b) - Schedule takes priority over maintainability characteristics of software:

No extended return will happen because generalization of system components will be curtailed or prevented in an effort to get something out the door quickly. Modifications to the installed system will cost above industry norms.

6 - No usability lab, very "techy" error messages:

Graphical and visual display workstation system components will not have extended return. Potential loss of user rapport and good will because of less than human displays.

7 - Bugs are fixed by extensive unpaid and un-documented overtime rather than prevented by budgeted walkthroughs:

The quality of the original architectural choices will degrade over the long term as quick patches destroy the original integrity of the design. Extended return will diminish over the long term and give stretched out return on investment. Also, because of lack of bug prevention practices, there may be no extended return at all since people will suspect the original design is buggy due to poor engineering practices and therefore decline to use the components.

8 - Programmers write user documentation if they can get around to it.

Marginal extended return. Programmers typically write poorly and that will affect the readability of the documentation. Poor readability irritates the user community so they fail to support future extended return costs because of irritation with initial system. Quality documentation at both user and developer level is mandatory (but for differing reasons) if system components are to be passed on to the next new system.

9 - Bugs not traced back to locate the development phase in which the bug originated:

Developers handle the initial project but are unable to deal with larger Good Stuff projects due to inability to review current process and thus learn from mistakes.

10 - A business user representative not on the development team:

Poor, difficult-to-use graphical and visual display system components. High risk of not finding business procedure components having extended return.

11 - No detailed historical record keeping for code repair costs:

No one will be able to tell that Good Stuff was really a success because there is no base for comparison. Arm waving about success will be met with cynicism and therefore there will be little incentive to get behind future uses of Good Stuff. Interest in Good Stuff fades because people can't put their fingers on its success.

12 - Users present informal requirements to the team which uses them without further formal refinement:

Poor business procedure system components leading to systems which operate below expected convenience or accuracy. Costly rework required. Few such components having potential extended return get discovered.

13 - Team begins coding without doing formal design and architecture work:

Large systems suffer severe overruns, low or no extended return, modification costs higher than industry norms, high personnel burnout/turnover and a plague of miscellaneous other seemingly bad luck symptoms.

14 - No version control procedures:

No extended return because the component library (inventory) will be in chaos and therefore will scare off potential redeployment prospects. Difficulty in rolling back to a previously known good system version if a surprising bug appears.

15 - No useful company-wide naming practices for components:

No extended return because people can't easily remember or access the names of the available components that could be redeployed in subsequent systems. High maintenance costs because of low system understandability.

16 - No developer understanding of useful software design concepts:

Code will be hard to maintain with costs above industry norms. If the code was designed excluding Good Stuff architectural concepts, Good Stuff generically gets a bad name leading to long term rejection of Good Stuff.

17 - Efficiency of code is given continuous high priority throughout the development cycle:

Team will tend to produce all the code such that is not easily generalized. Universal focus on efficiency will thus raise overall system cost without commensurate playback. Return on investment is stretched out because of high cost of re-generalizing code for redeployment in future systems that do not actually need the efficiencies of the initial system.

18 - Upper management "renegotiates" developer work estimates:

Typically discourages developers from being alert for opportunities to exploit or create extended return components. But each developer will have some internal moral rule set about what to short change when schedules are perceived as unrealistic. It could be the items of quality (bugginess), function, maintainability or extended return. The risk is that you don't know which item, how much that item choice will bite later and how the combination of choices made by all the developers will perturb project success.

19 - No ongoing review of the company's software development process or no process at all:

Random adoption of Good Stuff confined to small projects or single individuals. No way to detect success from any kind of improvement even if it was magnificent. Non-technical management loses control of software again after an initial flurry of success.

20 - Upper management perceived as disinterested in developer problems:

Long-term fade of interest in Good Stuff – treated as just another fad, or just another example of "you don't have to do what they say." Answers to the 10 high-payback questions become perfunctory and vague.

Glossary

The following terms are used with reckless abandon throughout this book. To aid the non-technical reader, these terms are collected here along with useful but not necessarily academically rigorous definitions. The definitions are intended to be adequate for comprehension of this book and will not withstand bludgeoning by purist theoreticians.

Occasional review of these words is also a way of building up your power vocabulary, making it easy to have the same kind of free-flowing conversation with your technical staff that you have with your sales staff. For greater detail, please see your friendly, neighborhood computer guru, who will be pleased to entertain you with the geek viewpoint on these things.

Alpha - the Essence term for the phrase we use in this book, namely, "core element of a software development process." We don't use the term "alpha" in this book anywhere else because it makes people's heads spin. It is included here in case you are a lurking theoretician. Essence defines seven core elements of a software development process: opportunity, stakeholders, requirements, software system, team, work, and way of working. They are described below and we will certainly use these element names many times elsewhere.

Analyst - a person who studies the context in which a business opportunity exists in order to capture the nuance of both the problems to be solved and the structure of possible solutions. Analysts rarely create or use components with extended return. But, when given explicit directive to do so, they can be invaluable allies in getting extended return by discovering common business patterns that occur across seemingly separate business activities. If they discover those patterns, no doubt they should be somewhere in line when the glory is passed around.

Architect - a key figure in the production of systems that have extended return. A key architect goal is to think out a high-level system design which will capture shared business behavior, shared communication or shared technology in such a way as to make its business value available to both current and future systems. In the terms of this book, an architect is a "creator" of extended return component designs. The architect has a major impact on the contents of the Software Floor Plan Diagram. The architect's activity requires exceptionally strong support from upper management. Good software architects are hard to find. The 10 great ones are a national treasure and don't work for your company.

Architecture - an expression of the planned use, style and long-term fit with a system's context. A system's components may be usefully assembled in many ways. An 'architecture' is a particular thoughtful way, a way with more goals than just the ones of a system's working in an error-free manner and delivering value at the required speed. Besides delineating system function, a major goal of your team should be to craft an architecture, at an early time, which reveals both the risks of the system, the adaptive character for future change and places having potential for extended return. Another goal is to preserve and utilize the extended return from earlier systems.

Artifact - anything tangible created by a software team during a project which is a necessary part of the process of getting the software end product itself. Often, the artifact uses some form of paper as its media, but electronic media are popular too. A Software Floor Plan Diagram is one example of such an artifact and its representation could be on paper, whiteboards, Web pages, slides, etc. In the bad old days, code was considered the only useful artifact. Discarded pizza cartons don't count.

Coder - another name for developer or programmer, but a name that is dated and sometimes seen as downscale, as in "He's just a coder."

Cohesion - a property of system components. A component is said to be cohesive if all its sub-elements can be shown to be organized towards a single precisely expressible goal, ideally a goal that can be expressed as a punchy verb acting on a precise business object. Cohesive components tend to also be ones that exhibit extended return potential. Why? If the goal has such precision, it is highly likely that it was important enough in the past (or present) to warrant such precision in order to ensure there would be no mistake in its application to business progress. That history speaks well for its future utility. A Swiss army knife is not cohesive. A steak knife is.

Compiler - a piece of software that runs on a computer and translates programmer code into something which can be run on a computer as bits. Programmer code is rarely directly run on a computer; the code is first operated on by the compiler to produce bits. The translated bits then run in the computer. Got that?

Component - a sub element of the working system. A component does not have size in any fixed sense. A city could be said to be a component of a state. A house could be a component of a city. A door could be a component of a house. So, a component for a computer system could be something as small as a few lines of programmer code or as large as an intranet with all its subsidiary computers. Size depends on the context of discussions in which the phrase "whole system" is being used.

Coupling - a property of system components. Coupling refers to the complexity of the fitting or interface that exists between two or more components that are supposed to work together. Generally, designers aim for systems having components with simple interfaces as these have "low coupling." High coupling is undesirable as that usually means that the components are not easily redeployed since the implied interconnection complexity is not always readily reproducible or cost-effective in the new system. Components may also be highly coupled if they share assumptions about the business context. So, another effect of high coupling is that a change to one component mandates a change to any other component sharing that assumption. The shared assumptions compound any effort to modify, enhance or repair a system. The Software Floor Plan Diagram shows components and how they depend on one another. Such dependencies are the way coupling shows itself.

Creator - a person who designs, specifies, discovers or invents a component having extended return. Actually, anybody could potentially be a creator, but typically, architects, designers and often analysts have the formal responsibility. They probably get all the glory, too.

Design - to carefully think out how a problem's solution should be best expressed in computer code, before constructing the code. The design activity is given extensive resources in companies desiring extended return on software. It is given less priority in companies that need excitement and undocumented overtime.

Designer - a person who designs components. Compared to architects, a designer works at a lower level of detail and typically organizes components over a smaller scope. In terms of this book, a designer could be a "creator" of extended return components.

Developer - Another name for programmer, although the developer job description often includes design and analysis skills not expected from a "programmer". The term is considered a slightly more upscale term than "programmer" and substantially more upscale than "coder." "Developer" is used in this book to stand for a technician without regard to any specialization the technician may have in the areas of analysis, design or coding - in other words, any non-management member of the software team.

Extended Return - shorthand for the phrase "extended return on the initial software investment"; a highly sought-after goal, a desirable characteristic of system components, in fact, the Holy Grail. Generally, a component having extended return is one that has correctly captured a business value, procedure or technology which will be needed over the foreseeable future in a wide variety of new business opportunities. As important as the capture is, additionally, such a component has also been crafted to easily fit into the future computer systems needed for these new opportunities - so easily, in fact, that it becomes commonplace and routine to make them a part of the new systems (see Generalize). The "extended return" refers to the extended return on investment received above the cost of the component's initial creation and above its original utility in the first system in which it was used. Regrettably, extended return components do not spring up by themselves from the fan dust oozing out of the back of desktop computers. Rather, they need the more potent encouragement outlined elsewhere in these pages. Note: another term seen in the literature for this concept is "re-usability". We don't use that word here, because the term has gotten shop-worn and misses the financial point.

Executives (Top Level), CEO (Chief Executive Officer) - the people with the real power to improve software quality, reduce chaos, and get extended return if they enhance that power by unambiguously setting the appropriate priorities through the tactic of asking new questions at the right time. In terms of this book, they are crucial "supporters" of extended return, Essence and other Good Stuff.

Fitting - the mechanical plugs and electrical signal specifications which need to be common between two hardware components in order for them to work well together. Two pieces of software which are supposed to work together thus could be said to have a kind of "fitting" which they share. They also "fit well" if no adjustments or ad hoc modifications need to be made to either component during assembly into useful operation. "Fitting" is simply a less academic and more physically descriptive word than "interface" and thus may be more forceful in executive circles. See also Coupling.

Generalize, generalization (as in "generalize a component") - to think out the ways in which access to the procedures and features of a component may be made easy and more universal; then to adjust, rework and test the component to make sure the universality is reached. Generalization does not add features to the component. It is an attempt to make sure the component has sufficiently flexible fittings such that the component can be *assembled* into more than just the original system for which it was first created. For a component to have extended return in new systems, it must have both a utilitarian function for the new system and ease of assembly into the system. Generalization will be a new activity for developers and designers who are new to the goal of extended return. Generalization activities have a cost, which should be a formal part of the project budget.

Hysterical Optimism - a phenomenon of heroic programming. A team exhibits hysterical optimism when it behaves as if, against all odds, some software shortcut or short-changed process has a cost which will absolutely never show up as undocumented overtime.

Interface - An interface is a boundary between two things in contact. For software and hardware, the term is more frequently used as the notion of the specification for correct communication and data interchange between two or more software/hardware components. It is the thing which designers examine for high or low coupling. It is the communication between the boxes in the Software Floor Plan Diagram. See also Coupling.

Iteration - the repetition of some sequence of activities in the developer team's way of working. In software, the activities are plan, analyze, design architecture, design components, implement (often also called "coding"), integrate, test and assess. And in really heads-up companies, "generalization" is included somewhere in there. A completed iteration delivers an increment or piece of the full system's features including, importantly, the integration of that increment with whatever fraction of the system existed before the iteration was complete. There seldom is such a thing as too small an increment. Most popular software methodologies have some way of doing iteration or some idiosyncratic piece of jargon that means the same thing as iteration

Integration - testing whether two components, which are otherwise presumed to be functioning according to specifications individually, actually work together correctly in concert. While in theory one could integrate more than two components at a time, in typical software practice it is indulging in hysterical optimism to think you can get away with that. Integration can never begin too early.

Kernel - the Essence name for a collection of Alphas. We do not use this term in this book. It is included here to keep the theoreticians happy. The phrase is often seen in the literature as "the kernel will help you do..." which we find misleading because the kernel is an intellectual concept, that, in itself, cannot 'do' anything, including improve software. The kernel, and all of Essence, for that matter, is a thinking tool. The kind of grammatical shorthand quoted above leads to assertions without proof that turn off people who would otherwise be genuinely interested in improving software. It is definitely not recommended to say this word at company parties. You risk being thought of as fanatical.

Librarian - a person who provides the library, warehouse, distribution facility and advertising agency for extended return components. A librarian is in charge of software that is in "inventory." In terms of this book, the librarian is a key "supporter" of extended return.

Maintenance – repair activity to a system after it has been delivered to the user, usually in response to bugs and errors that the user detected. The addition of new features to a system is given a different name, generally "modification."

Model – a representation, generally in miniature, organized to show the approximate structure of something. The word "miniature" should not be taken to exclusively mean physically diminutive. In computer systems, it can mean smaller in amount or kind of detail, where the detail not shown has been intentionally omitted in order make what is being shown more accessible to easy discussion. The Software Floor Plan Diagram we spoke about earlier portrays selected aspects of a system's feature structure. There may be models of other aspects, for example timing duration, or the order that events occur in a system. No such model is more "accurate" or "better" than any other. Rather, each model may be thought of as more focused or specialized to aid progress towards some particular system construction goal.

Module - another name for component. Most people consider module as a specific name for a component that is a clump of programmer code, thus, it is likely a somewhat small component.

Opportunity - the set of circumstances that makes it appropriate to develop or change a software system, the reason you are doing it.

Programmer - the people most companies beat up on if a system is in trouble, when more likely, the fault was a design process that was short changed. Programmers implement a set of design specifications by writing code for components. In terms of this book, a programmer has the potential to be a "utilizer" of extended return components. The programmer title typically implies that the person writes code only and does not do system or component design as part of the job.

Requirements - what the software system must do to address the opportunity and satisfy the stakeholders.

Software Engineer - an oxymoron in companies not really practicing any formal software engineering disciplines or otherwise in a state of anarchy. An upscale term for programmer. A potential extended return component "utilizer."

Software System - the thing you pay all that money for. Also, historically, the thing the user swears at. Generally, a system is made up of software, hardware, and data that provides its primary value to the stakeholders by running, ideally, without error. Typically, it can be part of a larger software, hardware or business solution. Most of the time in this book, we simply say "system."

Stakeholders – the people, groups, or organizations that affect or are affected by a software system, for example, people who will derive benefit from the value of the delivered system or also could be just funders or requesters.

Supporter - a person who contributes to the preservation, distribution and general effect of making sure Good Stuff happens more than once. Political correctness is involved here, so managers count. The Olympic star supporters are ones that, in addition to their formal role in the effort, also encourage other people to become exponents of Good Stuff. Long-term supporters should absolutely get all the glory.

Team – the group of people actively engaged in the development, maintenance, delivery or support of a specific software system. The group most often tempted to indulge in hysterical optimism. It could be composed of a mix of end product users, architects, software engineers, coders, developers, programmers, analysts, testers, managers, librarians and, often, pizza delivery boys.

Tight Code - programmer code which has been explicitly written in such a way as to minimize the amount of computer resources needed to make the code perform its function in a very specific, real-time, operational context. Usually, tight code runs faster, uses less bandwidth or takes less storage space, but not all three at the same time. Usually, the specializations required for a specific context produces tight code that is not as easily reworked for new features or new business policies as would be code which is explicitly written to be more general or reconfigurable.

Utilizer - a person who redeploys a component from a previous system in a new system. The best way to make that happen is to give them access to supporter and creator roles. They actually want all the glory.

Version Control - the name of a formal activity which is designed to monitor and track changes in the specification and/or implementation of system components. All aspects of a system can be subject to version control - planning documents, design documents, code, test data, generalization etc. Version control practices are a requirement for extended return to occur. It is also an implicit part of knowing how the team's progress is going forward.

Walkthroughs - in its simplest form, walkthroughs are public peer review of any work product that is produced during the construction of a system. In real life, they can be informal or formal, elaborately structured or ad-libbed. A primary goal of a walkthrough is to reduce construction cost and repair or rework activity of the delivered system by catching errors before much construction has occurred. Walkthroughs are effective because of the same principle that makes it easier to tie your shoe before you trip over the lace rather than while you are on the ground having fallen on your face.

Way of Working - a typically team-specific set of practices and tools used by the team to guide or support their work. In the bad old days, we often called this a "methodology." But as time has progressed, various ways of working have acquired mixed case brand names which are proselytized and defended with great passion even though they are largely re-packaging of techniques by other names that hark back to the bad old days.

Work – activity involving mental or physical effort done in order that the team achieves the goals of producing the desired software system.

About the Author

Roland Racko has been an information technology consultant, lecturer, and instructor for more than 40 years.

He has helped software teams manage software success in Sweden, Germany, East Africa, Taiwan, Canada, and Fortune 100 companies in the United States. He has written columns for several computer trade magazines and his writings have been anthologized in two books.

One of his primary skills is ferreting out the issue behind a given apparent problem, and helping teams and executives understand in novel and useful ways what stops them from having the success they desire, and then leading them to take the necessary positive action steps.

Made in the USA
Columbia, SC
18 July 2017